International Conflict Resolution

International Conflict Resolution

Theory and Practice

Edited by

Edward E. Azar

*Director, Center for International Development &
Conflict Management and Professor of
Government & Politics, University of Maryland*

John W. Burton

*Director, Conflict Resolution Project,
University of Maryland and Co-Director,
Centre for the Analysis of Conflict,
University of Kent*

WHEATSHEAF BOOKS, SUSSEX

LYNNE RIENNER PUBLISHERS, BOULDER

First published in Great Britain in 1986 by
WHEATSHEAF BOOKS LTD
A MEMBER OF THE HARVESTER PRESS PUBLISHING GROUP
Publisher: John Spiers
Director of Publications: Edward Elgar
16 Ship Street, Brighton, Sussex
and in the United States of America by
LYNNE RIENNER PUBLISHERS, INC.
948 North Street, Boulder, Colorado 80302

© Edward E. Azar and John W. Burton, 1986

British Library Cataloguing in Publication Data
International conflict resolution: theory and practice.
   1. Arbitration, International 2. Pacific settlement
of international disputes
I. Azar, Edward E. II. Burton, John W.
   341.5'2   JX1952
ISBN 0-7450-0227-7

Library of Congress Cataloging-in-Publication Data
Main entry under title:

International conflict resolution.

    Papers from the inaugural meeting of the Council for
the Facilitation of International Conflict Resolution
held at the University of Maryland, June 1984.
    Bibliography: p.
    Includes index.
    1. Pacific settlement of international disputes —
Congresses. I. Azar, Edward E., 1938-   . II. Burton,
John W. (John Wear), 1915-   . III. Council for the
Facilitation of International Conflict Resolution.
JX4473.157   1986   341.5'2   85-30040
ISBN 0-931477-71-9 (lib. bdg.)

Typeset in Times 11/12 point by Alacrity Phototypesetters,
Banwell Castle, Weston-super-Mare, Avon

Printed in Great Britain by Billing and Sons Ltd, Worcester.

THE HARVESTER PRESS PUBLISHING GROUP
The Harvester Press Publishing Group comprises Harvester Press Limited
(chiefly publishing literature, fiction, philosophy, psychology and science
and trade books) Harvester Press Microform Publications Limited
(publishing in microform unpublished archives, scarce printed sources,
and indexes to these collections) and Wheatsheaf Books Limited (chiefly
publishing in economics, international politics, sociology, women's
studies and related social sciences); Certain Records Limited, and John
Spiers Music Limited (music publishing).

Contents

The Contributors

Edward E. Azar is Director of the Center for International Development and professor of government and politics at the University of Maryland. He has been engaged in AID-sponsored work in Lebanon where he served as an advisor to the Lebanese government. Born in Lebanon, Dr Azar has co-authored books on Lebanon and written a great deal on the relationship between development and conflict resolution.

Michael H. Banks is a lecturer in international relations at the London School of Economics, and a founding member of the Centre for the Analysis of Conflict. He has taken an active part on the councils of the Conflict Research Society and the International Peace Research Association, endeavouring to relate theory to the interests of those who focus on current problems. He has been visiting professor at the University of Southern California and at Dartmouth College. His *Conflict in World Society: A New Perspective on International Relations* was published in 1984, and forthcoming is *Resolution of Conflict: A Manual on the Problem-Solving Approach*.

John W. Burton is Director of the Conflict Resolution Project at the Center for International Development at the University of Maryland and initiator and Co-Director of the Centre for the Analysis of Conflict at the University of Kent, Canterbury. Once in charge of the Australian Foreign Department, Dr Burton taught at University College, London and the University of Kent and has written ten books on the theory of international relations with a special emphasis on means of change and of conflict resolution.

A. J. R. Groom is a Professor in international relations at the University of Kent at Canterbury and a founding member and Co-Director of the Centre for the Analysis of Conflict which is now based there. His written works seek to relate strategic thought to conflict resolution.

John W. McDonald is a lawyer, US career diplomat and former international civil servant who has specialized in multilateral diplomacy. He has spent twenty years of his career in Europe and the Middle East and last served abroad in Geneva, Switzerland, where he was Deputy Director general of the International Labor Organization, from 1974-8. Since 1978, as Special Negotiator for the State Department, he has held the rank of Ambassador on four separate occasions when he represented the United States government at global United Nations conferences in the economic and social fields.

Anthony D. Smith is reader in sociology at the London School of Economics. He is the author of a large number of books and articles that relate to social change and nationalism: *Theories of Nationalism* in 1971, *The Concept of Social Change* in 1973 and others, and more recently *The Ethnic Revival* in 1981 and *State and Nation in the Third World* in 1983.

Bryant Wedge was Director of the Center for Conflict Resolution at George Mason University of Fairfax, Virginia. He has taught psychiatry at the University of Chicago and Yale, and diplomacy at the Fletcher School of Law and Diplomacy and the Foreign Service Institution of the State Department, and international communications at Fairfield University.

Acknowledgements

This book was the direct consequence of the inaugural meeting of the Council for the Facilitation of International Conflict Resolution held at the University of Maryland in June 1984. We wish to express our appreciation to those sixty scholars who attended and made a contribution to thought in this emerging discipline and profession of facilitated conflict resolution. The chapters in this book rest heavily on their observations.

The support given us by the University of Maryland, and in particular by the Members of the President's Club, has made this and other publications possible.

We have been helped in writing this publication by Betty Nathan whose editorial skills will be appreciated by the reader.

Introduction

This book on the theory and practice of international conflict resolution is written to bring to attention new developments in this field.

The hopes of the early part of the century that disputes could be resolved by international courts were destroyed by World War II. Hopes that the United Nations could prevent and manage conflicts between nations were in vain, for those that were within member states were outside its jurisdiction, and those that were inter-state were subject to a veto in conditions in which both the Soviet Union and the United States perceived an advantage in backing one side or the other of a dispute.

However, in the last few years there have been significant advances in the understanding of the behaviour of nations, and, arising out of this, the development of processes of conflict resolution that appear to be acceptable to parties to disputes, and effective in resolving conflict. It is not too much to suggest that there is now evidence of a breakthrough toward means of resolving conflicts between nations, even protracted conflicts, in place of trying to manage them by threat, force or peace-keeping measures. In addition to making a contribution to the resolution of the sixty or so conflicts within and among small states, this may prove to be an important step toward resolving the many problems that affect adversely Soviet-US relations.

There have been major changes both in the theory and in the practice of conflict resolution at all social levels in the last decade or so. While the changes took place first in the domestic field, for example, in family relations, industrial relations and communal strife, in some important respects the theory which has evolved in the international field helps to explain and to

improve practice at the domestic level, which evolved prag-
matically.

In the first chapter Michael Banks points out how traditional thinking in international relations leads logically to threat
and deterrence systems. Not only is it negative in its applications, but it provides no basis on which to build positive
policies of conflict avoidance and resolution. It is a powerful
chapter and is a challenge to the international relations
scholar. It is, nevertheless, basic reading for those who wish to
understand why it is that world society has arrived where it is
— conflictual and with no institutionalized means of resolving
conflicts peacefully.

Then follow three chapters which deal with the theory of
conflict resolution within a theoretical framework that is an
alternative to the traditional one which Michael Banks has
outlined. Chapter two, by Edward E. Azar, reflects, in ten
propositions, the lessons learned after fifteen years of monitoring world events. From this empirical base he confirms the
findings of Banks. Chapter three, by John W. Burton, traces
out the changes that have occurred in the handling of conflict
since the United Nations was founded in 1945. It points to the
shifts that have taken place as a result of experience and places
these within a theoretical framework. Chapter four by Bryant
Wedge deals with the psychological dimension that traditional
thinking, based on 'state interests', seemed not to take into
account.

The alternative theory, with which this book deals, is based
on identity groups rather than the state as the unit of
explanation of conflict and the means of handling it. This
theory raises some interesting questions. Is ethnic identity
more important politically than nationalism? What is nationalism? Are ethnicity and nationalism and class all in their own
ways sources of identity? These are dealt with in chapter five by
Anthony Smith who takes an historical and behavioural
approach.

The next chapter, by A.J.R. Groom, deals with the
alternative process of conflict resolution, problem solving. It is
followed by an outline, by John Burton, of the procedures
associated with this approach. These processes are relevant to
great power relations and in chapter eight Edward Azar and

John Burton discuss the relevance of problem-solving processes, and the theoretical framework from which they spring, to Soviet-US relations.

The various threads are drawn together by Edward Azar by taking the case of Lebanon with which he has been directly concerned. This must be regarded as a test case: a test of theory and of practice.

In a final chapter Ambassador John McDonald makes his comments on the preceding ones. The link between theory and practice is important for each. The link between applied theory and formal diplomatic processes are also important to each. Indeed, unless theory, applications of theory and formal practice are worked on together there is likely to be limited progress made in this important field.

Little by little a library is now accumulating of books on conflict resolution — as distinct from traditional conflict settlement by judicial, mediatory and bargaining techniques. We have included, in addition to references at the end of each chapter, a selective bibliography at the end of this book. The book has been written for the student and the general reader. The short bibliography will provide further reading for those who wish to delve deeper into the history and theoretical origins of this strand of thought.

Edward E. Azar
John W. Burton
Editors

1 The International Relations Discipline: Asset or Liability for Conflict Resolution?

*Michael Banks**

This paper seeks to place the growing discipline of international conflict resolution in the wider context of international relations theory.

There are two themes that I wish to put forward. First, I am convinced that there is a pattern in the development of international relations thinking and research. It has culminated in what I shall call pluralist thinking. This involves very considerable shifts of attitude by comparison with ten, twenty, or fifty years ago in the study of international relations. If we consider international relations as a whole — as a body of thought over the centuries, as a collection of research findings, as a conventional wisdom, as a set of disciplined propositions about the world and the way it works — then we find that a message is waiting for us. It is a distinctive message about behaviour in the world, and *ipso facto*, about how to approach and analyze conflict.

The second theme is that there is a developing gap between theory and practice. The discipline is emerging as a critique, a sort of alternative international politics to that which actually goes on in the real world. There is a disjunction between what the academics say and what the practitioners are doing. This presents questions for us. How clear-cut is what we have to say? How useful is it? How practicable is it? How solid is it?

*This chapter is based on research funded by the Economic and Social Research Council (ESRC), reference number E00 242020.

5

Are we speaking in ideologies? Are we just presumptuous social scientists meddling in the real world to express our own values? Or are we actually implementing ideas which have in fact a firm intellectual basis?

If we ask the question, 'What is the relationship between theory and practice?', then there ought to be three possible answers, or at least two clear-cut answers plus one complex one.

One possible answer to the question is that practice dominates theory. On this view, the job of the academic is to be passive: to record what the practitioners do in the real world. We are basically archivists. We inductively store and retrieve, in some sort of ordered form, a record of the actions of decision makers. If we believe that practice dominates theory our job is to note what goes on, then sort it into patterns and when an inquiry is made to stand ready to report and explain what has been happening in the world. That is a positivist view of the relationship between theory and practice. It is objectivist. It is empiricist. It is, I think, a comfortable position — as long as one does not think too deeply about what the implications of it are, because it is based on a questionable assumption. That assumption is that it is possible to paint an accurate picture of reality, avoiding all wishful thinking and prejudice, simply by being a bystander who tracks down what has been happening, takes note of it, and imposes order on the data.

The reverse position in answer to the question 'What is the relationship between theory and practice?' is that theory is more important than reality. Now, unlike the objectivist-positivist position which is popular in the United States, this position has a long tradition in Europe. It is very widely held there now. It is certainly much more influential in Britain today than it was twenty years ago. The argument here is simply that men make their own history, and that they do this on the basis of ideas and passions: their ideologies, their values, their belief systems, the theories they hold about cause and effect. People in politics are trying to teach each other lessons all the time on the basis of their own commitment and understanding, within general world views, of current issues in politics and society.

Now, doing research on that assumption is very different

from the positivist position because it is subjectivist. We are not studying what people do. We are, instead, studying what people *think* they are doing. That, of course, is much more difficult. It creates a far more activist role for the academic because the focus is on ideas rather than institutions and policies. The creation of ideas is, of course intellectual activity. It belongs, therefore, in the domain of the academic and of the thinker. It means that we cannot stand back and be dispassionate archive keepers, because we are participants. We are all in politics, and that means that all disciplines are to some degree themselves political. They are a part of the world that we live in . They helped to create it, and now sustain it. As scholars in international relations, we are all contributors to the ongoing formation of politics in the world. That is a very extreme position, of course, one that is sometimes known as the structuralist position.

Both those positions, that practice dominates theory, and that theory dominates practice, should be treated as ideologies. They are extreme positions, and most middle-of-the-road academics take a compromise position: one that is less self-assured. They say: on the one hand, we cannot be wholehearted positivists because there are lots of well-known problems in that position. We have to modify it a bit. On the other hand, we cannot be wholehearted subjectivists either, because we are forced to recognize that there *is* a real world out there. There are decision makers, and military-industrial complexes, and jingoistic nationalism, and powerful economic forces. The crises are happening and we need to know about them. So what we must conclude on the theory-versus-practice question is that a moderate position is inevitable, rather than one of the two extreme positions.

This conclusion sets the context for an activist approach to work in conflict resolution. There is indeed an international relations system out there, and its institutions and organizations are real enough. But the real world is also made up of habits and practices and theories of how it all works. The theories are, to some degree, self-fulfilling and self-perpetuating. They help to create the reality that we have to deal with. We do need to recognize that the existing system is shaped and conditioned by ideas. As writers and teachers, we may not be responsible for making policy, but we are most certainly responsible for creating and maintaining the climate of opinion within which policy is made.

The lesson to be drawn from looking at the theory/reality relationship is that this real world of ours is not inexorable. If it was made by people, it can in principle be remade by people. The moral for conflict resolution as an intellectual movement is that we are in the business of reformist interventionism. We need to inject ideas into the international political system and its subsystems in order to unmake and replace some of the institutions, habits and practices which our own ancestors and predecessors have helped to instill and to reinforce in the real world. Not just in practical terms, but intellectually as well, there is an opening here. There is an ecological niche for conflict analysts, if we can take possession of it and use it in a way that is academically sound and socially responsible. Our values are those which we set for ourselves and which we are prepared to defend by reference to our knowledge of human aspirations and behaviour.

This means that we can take a semi-optimistic position. International politics presents a truly awful set of facts. Studying it is like working in the pathology department of a hospital. The positivist position, for that reason, is fatalistic and depressing — recording mainly horrid events. The structuralist position, in contrast, is unduly optimistic because its exponents have their own Utopia which they try to force upon everyone else. We cannot be either that optimistic, or that arrogant, but we can be semi-optimistic. There are opportunities for us to act. Put that way, the argument sounds modest and bland. When we look at its implications, however, in relation to the recent history and development of international relations theory, we find that it is actually bold and dramatic.

I want to turn now to the history of ideas in international relations, in order to show that a description of the situation we now find ourselves in requires a strong vocabulary. It includes the words contradiction, anomaly, crisis and paradigm shift. We are in a changing discipline, and today I am more confident about what scholars have to say than I have ever been before.

I would argue, when looking back over the history of

thought in international relations, that our discipline, in our century, has undergone a lengthy flirtation with empiricism. Empirical work has succeeded. It has produced findings, and explanations of a sort, and even intuitive insights. But these very successes are forcing us away from empiricism. Having passed through a phase in which facts have dominated theory, the logic of our scholarship is carrying us into a phase in which theory dominates facts. In this new situation, we have not just an opportunity but an obligation to criticize and to prescribe. At the same time, we need to accept fully the moral and political responsibility that we could safely, in the past, deny as long as we claimed 'scientific objectivity' for every statement.

To justify this argument, I must survey the evolution of thought in the field. There have been three so-called 'great debates' which have arisen during the history of the discipline. First, there is the realist v. idealist debate that has permeated the last four centuries. Second, there was the brief behaviouralist-traditionalist debate of the 1950s and 1960s. Third, there is the inter-paradigm debate of the recent past, the 1970s and 1980s. To refer to these is simply a way of organizing the material chronologically. When one looks back at all that has ever been written and said, about international relations and how the system works, it becomes apparent that these three debates encapsulate the major issues. I consider each of them in turn and then review the present situation of the discipline.

The debate between the realists and idealists is classical in the sense that it goes all the way back to the medieval diplomats and religious theorists. It goes back to the Westphalia Settlement of 1648 which formalized the institution of sovereignty and formulated the state system as a set of ideas (Nardin, 1983, pp. 57–62). It goes back to the notion that there are governments which have total control over their peoples, but must do business with each other even while each retains separate responsibility for security in a system that has no world authority. It goes back to the cynical relationships of the great dynasts of the seventeenth and eighteenth centuries in Europe. They created the world of power politics and its associated theory that has been so important ever since. The realist-idealist debate goes back also the natural law tradition: to the philosophers of the middle ages and the seventeenth-

century who created the ideas which lie behind our present
thinking about such issues as just war, human rights, human-
itarian intervention, justice and decent conduct between
groups of civilized people.

These philosophers, thinkers, lawyers, practitioners, and
proto-scholars produced fundamental theories and doctrines
about international politics which remain important today. In
particular they made three observations which have conditioned our understanding down to the present time.

First, they noted that we live in a condition of international
anarchy: there is no world government. This creates conflict
between states, because states are in a competitive position.
They then spun out elaborate theories about what this circum-
stance implied for the conduct of foreign policy.

But second, they noticed that we also live in a world of
cooperation and law. This is so, not because of any inherent
altruism in human nature, but because of the doctrine of
sovereignty. Sovereignty is a claim: 'This is mine'. To make
any claim in society is to concede a reciprocal obligation. In
practice this results in a network of rights and obligations,
expressed in law. Effectively, it creates a world-wide community of sovereign states. The community is limited, but its
implications for the interpretation and practice of politics are
far reaching (Mayall, 1983).

Third, the classic writers noted that states were not the only
politically significant features of the world. There was also a
latent unity of mankind even though it was both subjugated by
the sovereigns and split apart by the state system.

Out of those three observations, three schools of thought
and three quite distinct traditions of thinking about international politics grew into existence. The first contained thinkers who believed that the anarchy was what mattered. In their
view, from the competition between states everything we
needed to know of importance about international politics was
observable. These were the people we know as 'realists'. The
second group, by contrast, emphasized inter-state community.
They stressed the enforced, reciprocal set of obligations between states: the cooperative relationships. These were the
people who came to be known as liberals or 'idealists'. Third,
there were the people who emphasized global unity. For them,

shared humanity, however interpreted, counted for more than the integrity of the states. These included the people who became truly creative thinkers, revolutionary thinkers, radical thinkers: people like Karl Marx who thought about social class, people like Immanuel Kant who contemplated the destiny of the human spirit and its implications for politics, and many others.

The scholarly community is still divided among these three attitudes, and most of us find a home in one of them. Of the exchanges between them, the realist–idealist debate is the most significant because it gave us structures and institutions which still operate. It also endowed us with a durable vocabulary, some of which has become extremely damaging. Such notions as reason of state, balance of power, and national security dominate our thinking and cripple our creativity.

It is unfortunate that we seem to have retained the worst of the realist–idealist argument and lost the best part of it. The main division between the schools of thought reduced itself, in essence, to sterile argument about whether human beings are naturally conflictual or competitive. We may never know that, and certainly we do not know it now. All that we can observe is that in practice people exhibit both tendencies. The proper focus for the debate is, therefore, the conditions under which people are conflictual or competitive. Modern social science has sought this understanding which, I suggest, transcends the traditional discourse, and can give us some assistance in our task of looking at conflict resolution.

The best part of the old debates was the rich set of insights produced by the balanced nature of the exchange between the liberals on the one hand, and the realists on the other. The liberals insisted upon a full consideration of norms, values, morality, ideology, reform, law, progress and peaceful change, along with all of the concepts and proposals put forward by the realists. But this entire set of liberal–progressive–idealist ideas has been neglected in our own time.

In the years between World War I and World War II, there was a brief period in which the liberals, or Utopians as they were often (wrongly) called at the time, dominated thinking as a result of reaction to the disaster of World War I. The Great War had called into question the old mechanisms of international politics: alliances, arms races, secret treaties, and the closed diplomacy of the old élites. Theories of stable equilibrium, crisis management and great power hegemony went out of fashion.

A similar pattern, but reversed, occurred in the aftermath of World War II. That war destroyed faith in all the liberal analyses and prescriptions.

Our task now is to redress the balance. But constructive ideas in our time will need to have a more secure foundation than those which were so much discussed and to some extent implemented in the 1920s and 1930s: collective security, open diplomacy, majority voting, economic sanctions, intellectual cooperation, and all the rest. It was too easy for those fragile institutions to be discredited by Hitler, the Japanese military and the Italian Fascists. When we look back over this meandering river of thought which has been so heavily influenced by real world events, particularly the dramatic events of major wars, we can see the risks involved in the changing fashions. John Burton's *Dear Survivors* (1982) now suggests that only the prospect of another traumatic event — nuclear war — might enable us to accept a really progressive theory and, therefore, improve the practice of international relations.

The controlling ideas today are a legacy of the 1940s and of the 1950s, when we switched completely from liberalism to realism. That period was an intellectual disaster zone. If we look back at those Cold War decades and examine the way international relations was studied then, especially in Britain and in the United States, three particularly distressing features of it stand out: it was a period of realist dominance, without any liberal balance, and without the refreshment of radical thinking.

If we spell that out specifically, we can see what happened. Consider the intellectual capacity of realism to explain the world, to predict it and to provide prescriptions that would enable decision makers to control it and to deal with problems. Individually, scholars knew that capacity to be well short of 100 per cent. But collectively, we allowed the policy-relevant utility of realism to be overrated and distorted. There was no full-scale criticism of it from a liberal perspective. There were no major liberal spokesmen. There were no influential books written by liberals, idealists, Utopians, reformists, progressives. The discipline had become intellectually totalitarian, dominated by one school of thought.

In addition, realist theory became intermixed with superpower ideology. Much of the work in international relations was a vested interest of those who advised the foreign policy establishments of the great powers, particularly in the United States. The comments of Stanley Hoffmann (1977) on this matter are interesting and powerful. Many scholars began to see it as their job to give advice to government on how to maximize the values that represented American interests in world politics: international order and stability, alliance cohesion, counter-insurgency, the effective use of military force and all the rest. These became major concerns in the discipline, but they are not explanatory theories of how the world as a whole works; they are merely the perceived policy needs of one status quo actor in a dynamic and complicated system.

Furthermore, conformism meant that we lost the stimulus of the revolutionists, the people who saw visions of what might be in world politics, the thinkers who were so subversive of orthodoxy in previous centuries. Consider the sheer quality of some of the old radical thinking. We had the integration theory of such people as David Mitrany in the inter-war period. We had the great classical works of Schumpeter and Hobson, Marx and Lenin, Mill and many others on social structure, class systems, imperialism and foreign policy. We had the work of Rousseau and of Kant on the nature of peace, or their more gentle equivalent in St Pierre and the Quaker/pacifist tradition. We had the medieval just-war theologians, pondering moral obligation, decency and civilized conduct.

All these were ignored in the 1950s and 1960s. Instead we put our minds to supposedly key questions such as, 'Are we more safe in a bipolar world or a multipolar world?' We studied escalation in nuclear warfare. We analysed all the things that were wrong with the United Nations, and why individual persons could not be subjects of international law. Our training was in a field that had lost the humanism and breadth of the classic writers in international relations. It had instead become narrow and, in a real ideological sense, self-serving — a travesty of the great tradition of international relations.

I come now to something more technical, the second of the great debates, traditionalism v. behaviouralism. This occurred in the 1950s and 1960s, mainly in the United States, but also in Western Europe. It consisted of an attempt by a 'Young Turk' movement to make international relations more scientific, more professional, more effective. It resulted initially from the appearance of younger scholars in the discipline who were true professionals, the first generation to be trained in it. There was also a powerful impact from the behavioural movement in other branches of social science. The new arguments were not concerned with values and policy implications, as the realist–idealist debate had been. They were concerned with methods, with proof, testing, with the structure of theories, and with the quality of explanations that could be regarded as satisfactory in international relations.

This second 'great debate' produced a great deal of contention. There was a very sharp division in the field from the 1950s to the 1970s. Despite protests from the traditional side, there was a wave of scientific research inspired by the vision of positivism that I referred to earlier. There was energetic use of quantification, systematic data gathering, computer work and simulation. Elaborate new theories were put forward, stimulated by vigorous interdisciplinary activity that introduced new concepts and analytic frameworks. The whole would-be revolution created extravagant hopes: we could have a positive value-free science. We could have a unified social science in which the entrenched distinction between international relations and domestic politics would disappear.

Today that second great debate is over. Through the corrective lenses of the post-behavioural period, we can see that behaviouralism was at its peak about twenty years ago. It was not a failure, but its success was very functionally specific. It was a genuine debate, clearly, because it clarified important issues. It taught us things that we had never considered before, things that we needed to know about methodology and research techniques. It introduced novel categories of analysis in international relations — perception, system, decision — and for those alone, I suggest, it can fairly be called a revolution.

But it was not the most important of the historic debates in the field. As time goes by, it seems rather less important, even undesirable, because it diverted the central focus of the discipline. That focus should be on general theory: on how to build a constructive vision of the world as a whole and the way in which it all fits together. Consider for a moment the decades of the 1950s, 1960s and 1970s and recall what students read in their textbooks, what professors said in their lectures, and what we all thought we knew about the world in each period.

In the 1950s we all *knew* what the world was like. We talked in a confident way about international politics and how to interpret conflict and other things within that framework. We had our nice solid theory of power politics and sovereignty, summarized in Morgenthau's famous text (1948). We thought that in a very broad way, we could predict events and understand them. Then came the behavioural revolution. Its immediate effect was that we dropped that general theory, and, in the 1960s, nothing officially replaced it at all. We all had a creed. We were going to have open minds and a thousand flowers were to bloom. We would look for ideas in psychology and anthropology and biology. We would test everything we said, which meant we had to operationalize our propositions and thus make them specialized and technical.

The result was that instead of having a general view of the world, we had little fractions of ideas which we came to call 'islands of theory'. The point about islands is that they stand in an ocean, in this case an ocean of ignorance. Although the behaviouralist credo of precision, rigour and the systematic use of quantitative data was in itself wholly admirable, it prevented us from making generalized assumptions about the world at large. So, as we moved from the 1960s to the 1970s, beyond the behavioural attack on the old mainstream thinking, we found ourselves with no general theory at all — or at least none that leading scholars would admit to.

That situation was both unfortunate and unreal. It was unfortunate because people in the discipline, recognizing this problem, stopped talking about the world as a whole. Instead, the discipline of the 1970s became one of specialists, diffuse and fragmented. A smaller and smaller proportion of all scholars in the field looked at the grand questions. This meant that their work, excellent though it often was, was conducted in a vacuum. There were numerous technical studies of arms control unenlightened by any deeper consideration of the larger problems of peace, war and security. Area studies burgeoned, producing a rich — but necessarily ephemeral — literature. Multinational companies were subjected to exhaustive analysis, but there was no comparable advance at all in the much more significant and lasting questions of fundamental political economy, involving the basic relationships between economic, political and social processes and their implications for the distribution of wealth and the achievement of security and human welfare. By the mid-1970s, it was very hard to find general theories in international relations at all. One paper (Phillips, 1974) captured the mood precisely: 'Where have all the theories gone?' In this respect, the effect of the behavioural movement was unfortunate.

Its effect was also unreal. The apparent loss of faith in the general theory of international relations was merely an illusion. It is simply not possible to talk about the world without having a general theory, however tacit or implicit. What really happened in the behavioural revolution was that the pre-existing dominant theory, realism, was not abandoned at all. It just went underground. We now have a magnificent study of that period, by John Vasquez, called *The Power of Power Politics* (1983). It is probably the best single product of the whole behavioural revolution, because Vasquez demonstrates beyond doubt that the behavioural 'islands' were actually linked to a continent of theory. Quantitative behavioural research was, of course, very fine work. It consisted of laborious, painstaking, Kuhnian normal science (Kuhn, 1962). It involved systematic gathering of information, precise specifying of hypotheses, exhaustive testing, careful exclusion of uncontrollable variables and so on. But what the behaviouralists did was to use, unconsciously in many cases, the realist paradigm to guide the research. Its achievement was to provide proof that the realist paradigm does not properly either describe or explain the world.

As Vasquez points out, we now must find a general theory that makes sense, fits together, and explains the data better than the realist paradigm did in that very long period of realist domination from E. H. Carr (1939) to Morgenthau (1948), in the 1940s and 1950s, and onward to the behaviouralists in the

1960s and 1970s. We now know that we need to have a better theory.

The search for a better theory forms the third debate. It was developing in the 1970s, and has become in the 1980s a major focus of attention among those people who take the risk of thinking about the general theory question. The debate is about what Kuhn called paradigms; those who do not like Kuhnian language about the structure of scientific revolutions can simply call them 'perspectives', 'frameworks', 'world views', or 'attitudes' towards world politics as a whole. They are emergent rather than fully developed. But they are certainly identifiable and the interchange between the schools of thought is potentially the richest, most promising and exciting that we have ever had in international relations. The three perspectives are: realism, still alive but only, I think, among people who have not read Vasquez and have not yet looked at the implications of his work; structuralism, also known as Marxism or dependency theory; and the world society perspective, or pluralism.

How did they emerge? Realism, as has been explained, has always been a part of the discipline. Structuralism has existed at least since the nineteenth century among the radical fringe, although many people (including some of the world's present leaders) studied in the great universities of the English-speaking world in the 1940s and 1950s without learning anything beyond a caricature of it. But it has been reinvigorated in the 1980s by dependency theory in the Third World, by 'world system theory' in the USA (Thompson, 1983), and by the resurgence of Marxist thinking in Britain and Western Europe.

Pluralism, however, is relatively new. It is possible to regard pluralism as a successor, in a direct linear sense, to classical liberalism. But I see it more as the product of the behavioural revolution because it is based on empirical findings produced in that very solid period of critical scholarship and quantification in the discipline. The findings consist of things that scholars have observed in the world, technical findings from technical studies which do not fit realism and cannot be explained by the old paradigm.

Thomas Kuhn, in his study of the structure of scientific

revolutions, has the right word for these vitally significant observations. He calls them 'anomalies', a term which aptly suggests the problems which are raised when something happens that does not fit a body of agreed propositions. An anomaly is inexplicable. Faced with it, one must either ignore it or change one's most fundamental assumptions. International relations today has, as we are only now beginning to realize, an unacceptable quantity of significant anomalies. Vasquez (1983, ch. 8), lists a large number of them, Burton's work has long been concerned with them (1965, 1968, 1972, 1974, 1982, and 1984), and there are useful overviews in two recent collections of papers, one edited by Maghroori and Ramberg (1983) and introduced by James Rosenau, and the other a set of essays in honour of John Burton (Banks, 1984).

The most perceptive scholars in the field, naturally, have been aware of anomalies for many years. Consider, for example, the work of Arnold Wolfers, the distinguished Swiss realist who taught at Yale. As far back as 1951, he mused upon the odd fact that intelligent, well-informed people can take such diametrically opposed positions as the liberals and the realists persistently do take on the question of the-state-as-actor. Was there, he asked, 'some unexplored terrain lying beyond their controversy?' (reprinted in Wolfers, 1962, p. 82). For him, it was right to treat states as 'billiard balls' — hard objects bouncing off one another on a smooth surface — because that conveniently simple assumption permits us to build plausible-looking theories. But what if states are not billiard balls? We can now see that Wolfers had the insight of a prophet, despite the fact that he himself had nothing further to add. It was left for others to enter the unexplored terrain, and different scholars have attempted it in different ways.

Initially, many of us thought that the most far-reaching benefits to be gained from exploring the Wolfers anomaly would be produced through foreign policy analysis. Like many of my peers, I was greatly encouraged by the appearance, in 1954, of the celebrated Princeton research paper on the decision-making framework (see Snyder, 1962, pp. 14–185). The new subfield, rapidly developed by a swelling coterie of researchers, raised a whole series of pertinent questions. What

do we find if we open up the billiard ball and inquire how
foreign policy is made within the state? Does the concept of
national interest still have a role to play? How do perceptions
fit in? In what way do domestic politics and foreign policies
interact?

An impressive body of work followed, and if we look back at
it from the perspective of 1984, there is genuine cause for
disciplinary pride because we now know some of the answers.
We know that states are not particularly rational actors, but
are better thought of as creatures of habit that learn slowly
(Deutsch, 1963; Steinbruner, 1974). We know that the external
postures of states are heavily influenced, to say the very least,
by the internal machinations of bureaucratic politics (Halperin, 1974). We know that subjective attitudes and false
perceptions play a major role (Jervis, 1976). Above all, we
know how complex and varied states can be in their behaviour
(Rosenau, 1980). The entire picture carries the message for us
that states are anything but unitary rational actors in the way
that realism requires them to be. On the basis of foreign policy
analysis, one of the central pillars of the realist paradigm has
come tumbling down.

But also we know that foreign policy analysis cannot itself
provide a better theory. Little work of significance has been
conducted in that subfield in the past decade. Clearly, it has
run out of steam. The reason is obvious, and it takes us back to
Wolfers: foreign policy analysis is imprisoned by its starting
assumption, that states are the principal actors in the international system. Maybe they are, but we cannot explain
everything that states do, still less everything else that happens in the world, if our analytic framework concentrates
exclusively on the means by which governments reach decisions. We must find some way of including the sources of
the pressures that so burden the practitioners of politics,
especially those that involve the risk and the activity of violent
conflict. We need to allow for actors other than governments,
for trans-national processes, for liberation movements, for
ethnicity and ideology. In the state-centric perspective of
foreign policy analysis, these matters are too easily over-
looked.

Exponents of the subfield are coming to recognize that their own past successes are now leading them back toward the need for a wider theoretical framework, as James Rosenau, for example, has noted (1980, p.3). There is an echo here, in Rosenau's call for a multi-actor analytic scheme, of J. David Singer's (Singer, 1961) famous recognition of the anomaly known as the 'levels of analysis' problem in international relations. As Singer shows so clearly, the state-centric focus of realism, with its primary concern being the explanation of government decisions, could never accommodate insights and theories derived from an exploration of processes at work on non-governmental levels of societal action.

Overall, it would seem that the most productive legacy of our Wolfers anomaly is to be found not in the foreign policy analysis field, but in the much less well-developed efforts of a scattered and uncoordinated group of pioneers to coax the general theory of international relations in a pluralist direction. In place of the billiard ball metaphor, they have substituted the image of the interconnecting cobweb (Burton, 1972; Mansbach, Ferguson and Lampert, 1976). Instead of the focus on decision makers, they have suggested that we concentrate our attention on the newly present (or perhaps just newly discovered) interaction patterns of economic interdependence (Morse, 1976; Keohane and Nye, 1977). Rather than continue to assume that security can only be achieved by the threat of force, they have put forward the idea — based on observed evidence — that integration may be an equally effective, perhaps much more effective, means of achieving the same objective (Lijphart, 1981, analysing the work of Karl Deutsch). Contrary to the realist doctrine that states are always masters of their own destiny where international law is concerned, they have begun to tabulate and spell out the contemporary existence of international 'regimes' involving collaboration and agreed procedures of a kind implicit in the naturalist legal theory written by Grotius 350 years ago (Krasner, 1983). Where the realist paradigm stresses the high politics of élite diplomacy, a few of the most daring pluralist thinkers (Burton, 1974; Alger, 1984) have begun to trace out the ways in which a participative, almost populist, form of international politics may be both possible and even beginning to happen. So far, all these contributions are piecemeal and incomplete. A full-scale synthesis is needed, perhaps building on the kind of scheme set out in Mansbach and Vasquez's *In Search of Theory* (1981). And given the continuing strength of the competition from the realist and structuralist devotees, there will no doubt be constructive criticism to help the synthesizing task along its way (e.g. Barry Jones and Willetts, 1984).

An anomaly of a very different kind was set before the discipline in 1966 by Martin Wight, a contemporary of Arnold Wolfers. 'Why,' he asked, 'is there no international theory?' (in Butterfield and Wight, eds., 1966, pp. 17–34). It was a sad paper. Like virtually all the prominent figures of his generation, both his academic conclusions and his emotional convictions held him firmly in a realist framework, but he fought to escape from it. For him, the word 'theory', when applied to society and politics, should properly mean political philosophy. He was no crude empiricist, and he bemoaned the coarseness of international relations theory: it was a body of knowledge concerned with means but not with ends. Power politics, he argued, was merely a theory of survival, not a theory of the good life. Why, he asked, can we not have a coherent political theory of a normative kind of world politics? What about justice, human rights and progress? Why can we not provide navigation points, beacons more constructive in their function than what he called the 'casuistry of reason of state' (p. 24), to help guide the decision makers?

Wight himself could not resolve his anomaly, falling back wearily on what he saw as 'the recalcitrance of international politics to being theorized about' (p. 33), and rejecting the argument that scholars should just go ahead and compose normative theory, with the harsh comment that 'it is surely not a good argument for a theory of international politics that we shall be driven to despair if we do not accept it' (p. 28). Luckily for the discipline and indeed for humanity at large, other scholars of the calibre of David Mitrany, John Hobson, Karl Deutsch, Quincy Wright, Richard Falk, Johan Galtung, Kenneth Boulding, Anatol Rapoport and many others have all — in different ways — implicitly recognized and acted upon the Wight anomaly without sharing his gloomy conclusion.

It is clear, then, that we have anomalies in plenty in international relations. Empirically, things have been happening in the real world that are not predicted by our existing theory; normatively, questions are being raised for which the theory has no answers. What can we expect in this situation? Kuhn is helpful on this point (Kuhn, 1962). He makes three predictions, based on his analysis of past revolutionary shifts in other fields of study. First, he suggests, anomalies are universally present; all disciplines have some and at all times, but they do not matter as long as they are neither numerous enough, nor significant enough, to undermine general faith in the discipline. Scholars can say: despite these anomalies, we have a useful paradigm, so we are going to carry on with what we are doing. Paradigms, in other words, are tenacious, not so easily shrugged off; they are world views that form part of the identity of the persons holding them. The stability and persistence of a well-founded theoretical base is, in any case, what makes normal science possible. If progress is to occur, paradigms need to be durable, and generally that is what they are.

Kuhn's second prediction of a discipline's response to the presence of anomaly follows from the first. If anomalies contradict existing assumptions, then mental health requires that the contradictions be accommodated. This is done by rationalization. We 'explain away' the irritating and embarrassing observations by all the methods with which we are so uncomfortably familiar: making exceptions, adding qualifications, ridiculing the alleged counter-instance, stretching the fundamental theory without abandoning it.

Take a look, for example, at today's average international relations textbook. It represents our collective wisdom. 'Dear student', it says, 'here is international relations. Basically it consists of power-politics theory, which specifies that the need for security makes states behave aggressively. Their aggressive behaviour forms stabilizing patterns which we call balances of power, and enables big states to dominate lesser ones, which is why all those obedient minor powers have signed the non-proliferation treaty. We know, dear student, that there are numerous exceptions to these propositions; we shall call them special cases. The theory predicts that law, morality, ideology, religion and similar social forces are unimportant, but they exist and so we have put chapters on them in our textbook anyway. You must understand, dear student, that states are inherently compelled to respond rationally to their national interests; but world politics is also subsystem dominant, which means that states often disobey that systemic imperative. Conflict, dear student, is caused by the clashing of state interests. However, much research has shown that international conflict spills over from domestic disputes, that is, conflict within states rather than between them, so we have included some discussion of that too. The whole system is, of course, essentially political and not economic, but so much fuss has been made about economic forces in recent years that we have included sections on interdependence, the North-South dialogue, energy and the multinationals. We, the scholars, perceive all the contradictions but we cannot resolve them; you, the student, must do your best.' It is small wonder that our subject tends to confuse its undergraduates. My judgement is that our tendency to add the anomalies to pre-existing theory, rather than to rethink the theory, has gone far enough.

The third prediction in the Kuhnian account of paradigm change is that any paradigm which is riddled with anomalies must eventually enter a crisis stage. It will then collapse. In due course it will be replaced by a new paradigm which accounts for the anomalies in a satisfactory fashion. Self-reform in this way, Kuhn points out, is painfully difficult to any discipline. Usually the reconstruction of basic ideas must come from new people, perhaps operating in new institutions. Choosing and testing the replacement paradigm is no easy matter, because paradigms are incommensurate. It will not be possible to assess the worth of any candidate aspiring to the throne of academic world politics by the only method that comes easily to most of us, namely the application of what we instinctively think of as 'realistic' tests. Our notions of what is and is not 'realistic' are fundamentally conditioned by our professional training in what we must now see as an outmoded set of ideas. Instead, following Kuhn, we must decide what are the most significant questions that our discipline needs to answer, and select from the competing ideas the ones which most persuasively deal with those questions. Only then can we proceed to build a normal science, testing and checking.

Can we do this? It seems that we will have to. As I have sought to demonstrate in this review of the academic study of international relations, we are not starting from scratch in our attempt to make a constructive contribution to the resolution of conflict. The discipline does have assets. Some are to be found in the classical tradition, especially on the liberal side of the realist–idealist debate and in the radical insistence that political consequences do follow from the common humanity of people everywhere. Other assets are to be found in more recent scholarship, especially among the writings of those researchers whom I have identified as pioneers (by implication if not explicitly) of the pluralist approach. And the most important assets are to be found in the specialized studies of conflict resolution itself, from the foundations laid by Boulding (1963) and Johan Galtung in his many papers in the early years of the *Journal of Peace Research*, down to the most recent work reported in Azar and Farah (1981), Mitchell (1981), Kriesberg (1983), Banks (1984), and many others.

The task, then, is to draw upon these assets. With them we can satisfy Martin Wight's criterion for progress: that any new perspective must be founded upon reason, because emotional impulse alone is not enough. Our assets provide the resources needed to undertake what Kuhn describes as 'the reconstruction of the field from new fundamentals, a reconstruction that changes some of the field's most elementary theoretical generalisations' (Kuhn, 1962).

But as I have also argued, the international relations discipline is today weighed down by heavy liabilities. This means that its scholarly output must be employed only with the greatest of caution when the purpose is to find a theoretical basis for conflict resolution. Ideologically, many writers on international relations hold status quo views. These views incline them more towards the partisan manipulation of a conflict than towards its impartial mediation, and discourage altogether any sympathetic inquiry into means for the achievement of justice. Intellectually, there is a pervasive rigidity of attitude which holds back the spontaneous creation of new ideas within the discipline. It also obstructs an open-minded discussion of ideas that originate outside it. Taken as a whole, the discipline has become a processor that is expert in the recycling of old analytic formulas to fit the succession of new problems presented by the real world.

These ideological and attitudinal handicaps are intensified by the theoretical precepts of realism which operate to the systematic disadvantage of any attempt to build a powerful theory of how to analyze and resolve conflicts. The most basic premise of realism stipulates that violent conflict between states must be assumed to be inevitable. From that premise it is logical enough to deduce that the chances of violence are reduced by preparation for it, and that stability will best be assured in a heavily armed world run by experts in the controlled use of force.

That basic premise must be challenged if progress toward a stable and peaceful world society is to be made. And that is why a pluralist theory of international relations is so important in the construction of a viable approach to peaceful resolution of conflict.

BIBLIOGRAPHY

Alger, C. (1984) Report of an address given in Yokohama in 1982, in *Global Conflict*, John W. Burton (1984) pp. 74–82.

Azar, Edward E. and Farah, Nadia (1981) 'The structure of inequalities and protracted social conflict: a theoretical framework', *International Interactions*, 7, 4 (September), pp. 317–35.

Banks, Michael (ed.) (1984) *Conflict in World Society: A New Perspective on International Relations*. Brighton: Wheatsheaf; New York: St Martin's.

Barry Jones, R.J. and Willetts, Peter (eds.) (1984) *Interdependence on Trial: Studies in the Theory and Reality of Contemporary Interdependence*. London: Frances Pinter.

Boulding, Kenneth E. (1963) *Conflict and Defense: A General Theory*. New York: Harper and Row.

Burton, John W. (1965) *International Relations: A General Theory*. London: Cambridge University Press.

Burton, John W. (1968) *Systems, States, Diplomacy and Rules*. London: Cambridge University Press.

Burton, John W. (1972) *World Society*. London: Cambridge University Press.

Burton, John W. (1982) *Dear Survivors*. London: Frances Pinter.

Burton, John W. (1984) *Global Conflict: The Domestic Sources of International Crisis.* Brighton: Wheatsheaf; College Park, Maryland: CID, University of Maryland.

Burton, John W. *et al.* (1974) *The Study of World Society: A London Perspective.* Pittsburgh, PA: International Studies Association.

Butterfield, Herbert and Wight, Martin (eds.) (1966) *Diplomatic Investigations.* London: George Allen and Unwin.

Carr, Edward Hallett (1939) *The Twenty Years Crisis.* London: Macmillan.

Deutsch, Karl W. (1963) *The Nerves of Government.* New York: Free Press.

Halperin, Morton H. (1974) *Bureaucratic Politics and Foreign Policy.* Washington, DC: Brookings Institution.

Hoffmann, Stanley (1977) 'An American social science: international relations', *Daedalus*, **106**, 3 (Summer), pp.41-60.

Jervis, Robert (1976) *Perception and Misperception in International Politics.* Princeton, NJ: Princeton University Press.

Keohane, Robert O. and Nye, Joseph S. 61977) *Power and Interdependence.* Boston: Little, Brown & Co.

Krasner, Stephen (ed.) (1983) *International Regimes.* Ithaca, NY: Cornell University Press.

Kriesberg, Louis (1983) *Social Conflicts*, 2nd edn.. Englewood Cliffs, NJ: Prentice-Hall.

Kuhn, Thomas S. (1962) *The Structure of Scientific Revolutions.* Chicago: University of Chicago Press.

Lijphart, Arend (1981) 'Karl W. Deutsch and the new paradigm in international relations', chapter 10 in Merritt, Richard L. and Russett, Bruce M. (eds.), *From National Development to Global Community.* London: George Allen and Unwin, pp.233-51.

Maghroori, Ray and Ramberg, Bennett (eds.) (1983) *Globalism Versus Realism: International Relations' Third Debate.* Boulder, CO: Westview.

Mansbach, Richard W. and Vasquez, John A. (1981) *In Search of Theory: A New Paradigm for Global Politics.* New York: Columbia University Press.

Mansbach, Richard W., Ferguson, Yale H. and Lampert, Donald E. (1976) *The Web of World Politics: Nonstate Actors in the Global System.* Englewood Cliffs, NJ: Prentice-Hall.

Mayall, James (ed.) (1983) *The Community of States: A Study in International Political Theory.* London: George Allen and Unwin.

Mitchell, Christopher R. (1981) *The Structure of International Conflict.* London: Macmillan.

Morgenthau, Hans J. (1948) *Politics Among Nations: The Struggle for Power and Peace.* New York: Alfred A. Knopf.

Morse, Edward L. (1976) *Modernization and the Transformation of International Relations.* London: Collier Macmillan.

Nardin, Terry (1983) *Law, Morality and the Relations of States.* Princeton, NJ: Princeton University Press.

Phillips, Warren R. (1974) 'Where have all the theories gone?', *World Politics,* **26**, 2 (January), pp.155–88.

Rosenau, James N. (1980) *The Study of Global Interdependence: Essays on the Transnationalisation of World Affairs.* London: Frances Pinter.

Singer, J. David (1961) 'The level-of-analysis problem in international relations', chapter 5 in Knorr, Klaus and Verba, Sidney (eds.), *The International System: Theoretical Essays.* Princeton, NJ: Princeton University Press, pp.77–92.

Snyder, Richard C., Bruck, H.W. and Sapin, Burton (eds.) (1962) *Foreign Policy Decision Making.* New York: Free Press.

Steinbruner, John D. (1974) *The Cybernetic Theory of Decision: New Dimensions of Political Analysis.* Princeton, NJ: Princeton University Press.

Thompson, William R. (ed.) (1983) *Contending Approaches to World System Analysis.* London: Sage Publications.

Vasquez, John A. (1983) *The Power of Power Politics: A Critique.* London: Frances Pinter.

Wolfers, Arnold (1962) *Discord and Collaboration: Essays on International Politics.* Baltimore: John Hopkins Press.

2 Protracted International Conflicts: Ten Propositions

Edward E. Azar

I wish to set down ten related propositions on protracted social conflicts. These propositions have been generated by monitoring conflictual and cooperative events in world society over a decade. I will then show how these propositions throw light on conflicts generally and, also, on the theory and practice of conflict resolution.

I am using the term 'protracted social conflict' to suggest the type of on-going and seemingly unresolvable conflict that is our current concern, whether it be a conflict such as in Lebanon or Soviet–USA relations. I am not concerned with low-level conflicts which are part of the normal processes of change, and adjustment to it, which all persons and societies experience in relationships with others.

1. Protracted social conflicts have typical characteristics that account for their prolonged nature. In particular, they have enduring features such as economic and technological under-development, and unintegrated social and political systems. They also have other features that are subject to change, but only when conditions allow for far-reaching political changes. These include features such as distributive injustice which require the elimination or substantial modification of economic, social and extreme disparities in levels of political privilege and opportunity. Any 'solutions' that do not come to grips with these features are solutions that must rest on law enforcement, threat, or power control by the more powerful party to the conflict. Conflict is likely to erupt once again as

soon as there is any change in the balance of forces, in leadership, or in some other significant ecopolitical conditions.

2.   These observable features provide the infrastructure for intractable conflict: multi-ethnic and communal cleavages and disintegrations, underdevelopment and distributive injustice. The re-emergence of conflict in the same situation, a particular characteristic of protracted social conflicts, suggests to anyone monitoring events over a long period that the real sources of conflict — as distinct from features — are deep-rooted in the lives and ontological being of those concerned. Now and again this is confirmed in statements, as when some Turkish Cypriots once asserted that they were 'nameless people' because they could not issue their own passports. Those involved in protracted social conflicts seem to have difficulty in articulating what it is that leads them to violent protest and even war.

We are led to the hypothesis that the source of protracted social conflict is the denial of those elements required in the development of all people and societies, and whose pursuit is a compelling need in all. These are *security*, *distinctive identity*, *social recognition of identity*, and *effective participation* in the processes that determine conditions of security and identity, and other such developmental requirements. The real source of conflict is the denial of those human needs that are common to all and whose pursuit is an ontological drive in all.

3.   It is difficult to detect, to define and to measure a sense of insecurity and distributive injustice and other such deprivations. On the other hand, ethnic and communal cleavages and the political structures associated with them are more conspicuous. The fact that ethnic and communal cleavages as a source of protracted social conflicts are more obvious than others does not make ethnicity — used here to refer to identity groups that make up a polity — a special case. Ethnicity is an important case, though not a special one, because it draws our attention to a need that is fundamental. The study of ethnicity and the drive for ethnic identity enables us to understand the nature of conflicts generally. It is the denial of human needs, of which ethnic identity is merely one, that finally emerges as the

source of conflict, be it domestic, communal, international or inter-state.

4.   Situations of protracted social conflict in the world, of which there are more than sixty now active, are not unique events. To the participants — and to external observers who do not follow events over long periods — they appear to be unique, because local circumstances, histories and attitudes give them individuality. In fact, they are not accidental combinations of circumstances, but have certain behavioural and structural characteristics in common. They are predictable for this reason. Some conflicts may be accidental and short-lived — though tracking events suggests that there are probably few. Protracted social conflicts universally are situations which arise out of attempts to combat conditions of perceived victimization stemming from: (1) a denial of separate identity of parties involved in the political process; (2) an absence of security of culture and valued relationships; and (3) an absence of effective political participation through which victimization can be remedied.

5.   Tracking conflict, negotiations, temporary settlements and the outbreak of further conflicts (a sequence which is a characteristic of East–West relations no less than regional conflicts such as in the Middle East) draws attention to the reality that human needs and long-standing cultural values, such as those to which I have referred, will not be traded, exchanged or bargained over. They are not subject to negotiation. Only interests which derive from personal roles and opportunities within existing political systems are exchangeable and negotiable. Agreements that come out of negotiations that may give certain advantages to élites, but do not touch upon the underlying issues in the conflict, do not last.

6.   Conflictual and cooperative events flow together even in the most severe of intense conflicts. Cooperative events are sometimes far more numerous than conflictual ones even in the midst of intense social conflict situations. However, conflictual events are clearly more absorbing and have more

impact on determining the consequent actions of groups and nations. Cooperative events are not sufficient to abate protracted social conflicts. Tension reduction measures may make the conflict more bearable in the short term, but conflict resolution involves a far more complex process than mere conflict management.

7. The most useful unit of analysis in protracted social conflict situations is the identity group — racial, religious, ethnic, cultural and others. It is more powerful as a unit of analysis than the nation-state. The reason is that 'power' finally rests with the identity group.

I wish to deal with this proposition at some length, because in my experience this is the key to research and to conflict resolution.

For the purposes of describing, explaining and predicting the dynamics of a protracted social conflict situation, the identity group is more informative than the nation-state. Most nation-states in our contemporary international system are unintegrated, artificially grouped or bounded, and totally incapable of inspiring loyalty and a civic culture, despite the strength of nationalism and the sophisticated strategies of communication. This is a reality with which we must come to terms.

Since Westphalia, nation-states have been legal fictions of the international system. They perpetuate the myth of sovereignty and independence as instruments of control. There are times when national interest and group interest overlap, but these are becoming less obvious in the world.

Just as the rise of the nation-state since Westphalia has perpetuated the fiction that groups are not natural political units and will wither away and melt into the larger and more efficient and 'natural' unit, the nation, so has the rise of the individual in the last century perpetuated the fiction that all relevant political action deals with the satisfaction of all sorts of personal needs and wants of the discrete and smallest unit of social analysis, each separate individual. What is of concern are *the societal needs* of the individual — security, identity, recognition and others.

I realize that it is difficult for a student of international relations to get involved with empirical work on identity groups and their behaviour. The international institutions and system are biased in such a way that we often cannot find reliable data on ethnic or religious groups, whereas we do find data on national variables. Because some states are made up of apparently homogeneous groups and others are not, one experiences disincentives for comparative analysis. Our focus on nation-states and their individual actions has deflected our attention from the study of ethnic, religious and other identity group conflicts within these territorial entities.

The professional debate over the question of the appropriate unit of analysis has dwelt on the differences between focusing on the individual, state or system and their implications (Waltz, 1959; Singer, 1961). It has ignored the group totally. Our protracted social conflict research has impressed upon us the need to re-examine this issue of the unit of analysis and to correct this deficiency in the international politics literature.

The group appears to be a competitor to nation or system. Scholars in the field of international politics seem to have accepted the view that a legitimate role of the state is its historical role of suppressing the group. Furthermore, the group as a unit disturbs the neatness of the models at hand. We had no motivation to generate data and study the consequences of the actions of groups.

In my own work on events research and data banking, I took the most commonly accepted unit, the nation-state. My present familiarity with the phenomenon of protracted social conflict has led me to feel very strongly that we need to build data banks on ethnic, religious, cultural and other groups if we want to understand better the phenomenon of needs, interests and motivations of parties in protracted social conflict situations.

8.   Many internal and external relations between states and nations are induced by the desire to satisfy such basic needs as I have been describing. The unit of analysis is the identity group that makes this possible, be it the state, the nation or some more intimate group. The origins of international conflict are, therefore, in domestic movements for the satisfaction of needs

and in the drives of nations and states to satisfy the same needs. Thus, distinctions made between domestic and international conflicts are misleading.

I have argued earlier that groups as actors in protracted conflict situations initiate plans, actions, reactions and strategies in order to accomplish the goal of satisfying individual societal needs or of reducing and eliminating need deficiencies. For these purposes the domestic and the international are only arenas. In whatever arena the actors behave, they do so to satisfy their needs. The motivations for action are internal, not systemic or international.

Empirically, we have found that in protracted social conflicts actors seek to placate others, and seek alliances and do all the things they see as serving their interests, as they set out to accomplish the task of satisfying their basic needs. Of course, there are many other variables which affect the behaviour of groups and their leaders, but the basic motivation to act is internal, whereas the arena can be more extensive. In the conflict situations between 1979 and 1984 which we have examined, élites and their leaders show a serious contempt for international and regional arenas. They see these arenas as mere opportunities for scoring points with their own domestic constituencies. Self-image and perception of self by others are important needs to be satisfied, and, therefore, they can be a source for action and influence. In this sense, the regional and international environments are important, but only in a very limited way. Ultimately, actors behave in order to satisfy domestic social needs and not international ones.

To separate domestic and international is artificial — there is really only one social environment and its domestic face is the more compelling: thus, there are international and national interests which actors manipulate and exchange in return for the opportunity of satisfying domestic needs, but not the other way around.

9.   It follows that protracted social conflicts in multi-ethnic societies are not ameliorated peacefully by centralized structures. For conflicts to be enduringly resolved, appropriate decentralized structures are needed. These structures are designed to serve the psychological, economic and rela-

tional needs of groups and individuals within nation-states.

Traditional and contemporary political theory is weak in this respect. We have few models of decentralization that would ensure the pursuit of human and societal needs. Western political theory, for example, favours the centralized state and its legitimate monopoly of violence. In recent years attempts have been made to address the needs of minorities by human rights guarantees, as in the original Cypriot Constitution, and by 'power sharing', as attempted by the British government in Northern Ireland. Within the analysis I have made, neither could succeed. No compromises are possible when societal needs are at issue. We have to evolve non-power models.

The concept of a unified and centralized power entity has been mistaken for a socially integrated political unit. In protracted conflict situations, highly centralized political structures are sources of conflict. They reduce the opportunity for a sense of community among groups. They increase alienation and they tend to deny to groups the means to accomplish their needs.

Societies which have undergone decades of violence and hate retain very little trust for any sort of government — local or central and distant. They become cynical. They transform even benign systems into deformed political and economic entities and they show very little inclination to participatory politics. Decentralized political structures promise to provide the sort of environment which permits groups to satisfy better their identity and political needs. They promote local participation and self-reliance. They give the groups involved the sense of control over their affairs.

In general, decentralized political systems permit the local authorities control over their educational system and their social concerns. They increase the sense of identity, participation and security in the broadest sense of these terms. Decentralized political systems have shortcomings such as parochialism, they foster autocratic rule, they do not address inequality across regions and groups and generally tend to be inefficient. But the benefit might outweigh the costs. Conflict resolution in protracted conflict situations necessitates an understanding of the importance of open, participatory and decentralized political structures as opposed to centralized, dominant and exclusive structures.

It is here that international relations theorists have a contribution to make. The international system is governed on a functional basis, and is remarkably orderly. There are a large number of function agreements observed even in times of high tension and war. They cover communications, navigation, health, and even the treatment of prisoners in war. It is this functional model that could be applicable to situations such as in Cyprus and Lebanon, where each community seeks the security of its identity and independence, yet values its wider relationships within the state.

10.　My tenth and final proposition is that, not only have we been mistaken in taking the state as the unit of analysis in international relations and thus failed to perceive the continuity between domestic and international, but that we have, as researchers, failed to perceive the continuity over time of what appear to be discrete conflicts. I wish to communicate a perspective derived from monitoring events over a long period.

There is a strong tendency in international relations theory that leads us to regard conflict actions as discrete, delineated by time and space, and differentiated in terms of the actors, targets and issues involved. Conflict is thus perceived as a phenomenon found in the natural unity of action events which can empirically be isolated, formalized and studied. Each situation is seen as a unique one. No patterns or common features are related to common causes. The number of wars each year can be counted; but each one is taken as a separate event to be studied separately.

This is a confused point of view. What happens is that we the observers select events which we call conflict events and others that are not. We devise intellectual criteria to define conflict. It is important to emphasize that the set of events that we take as conflictual are always preceded and followed by a stream of events. The start and end points are established by the external observer, generally the researcher.

Furthermore, those events we designate as conflictual are also part of a set of observable relationships, economic, social and political 'cooperative' ones as well. We draw the conclusion that conflict is the result of a mix of factors, accidental and inevitable, a part of human organization, about which little can be done.

Because conflicts fluctuate in intensity over time, we tend to make assertions about starting and end points which may be of limited utility for an understanding of the inertia embedded in some conflict situations. Curves depicting change and stability in social relations over time may lead us to a poor understanding of the role of intervention, management and conflict resolution.

This view of the natural unity of the flow of events has led to a systematic omission of the notion of protracted social conflict from the domain of empirical research. I did not pay attention to this phenomenon of protracted social conflict until I began, as mentioned earlier, to look for patterns and to deal with the existential experience of Lebanon and the Middle East situation. Such conflicts linger on for a substantial period of time, sometimes interrupted by relatively low-level coexistence and even cooperation. On the other hand, they play a significant role in reshaping the societies involved, and have a considerable spill-over effect into the international society. (Burton, 1984).

We have thought that there are epoch-long changes involving social conflicts, and that the episodes which reflect the character of these changes are protracted social conflicts. However, when we try to formalize the beginning and end of these episodes which reflect the epoch-long phenomena, we find ourselves on very thin ice. The difficulty arises when we try to determine the start and end points and what we consider continuous, discontinuous or intermittent interactions. Does a conflict start at the moment of an act of aggression, at the installation of a conflict structure, or only at the moment of violent interactions? The main thing that we are finding useful at this stage of our intellectual development is that in studying protracted social conflict situations we benefit more from looking at historical sweeps of the episodes than from searching for specific starts or end points. This historical outlook is lacking in the recent traditions of political, sociological and social-psychological research on empirically based conflicts because of the dangers embedded in historiographic categories. Romantic overtones, which influence our impressions of these categories, have distanced social scientists from history.

CONCLUSIONS

What brief observations can be made on the handling of conflict situations from these propositions?

The outbreak of identity-related conflicts and crises has been on the increase since World War II, particularly in the Third World. Currently it is possible to identify more than sixty cases. Most are identity-related, that is, they involve tribal and cultural rivalries which can be traced to colonial boundaries and migrations. Examples are Lebanon, Sri Lanka, Northern Ireland, Ethiopia, Cyprus, Iran, Nigeria and Zimbabwe. The 'class struggle' is not a prime cause, though the existence of class itself creates conditions that promote identity struggles based on a common sense of deprivation and injustice.

Each conflict invites the intervention of great powers, thus complicating even further the relationships of those powers, and complicating, also, the already difficult ethnic relationships of each situation. The result is that all of these seemingly intractable and protracted conflicts exhaust the resources of those directly and indirectly involved, further deform the economy and thus accentuate underdevelopment. The increase of state-sponsored terrorism and the disruption of trade and commerce are a by-product of these conflicts, thereby making their resolution all the more important.

These conflicts appear to start with one set of stated goals, primary actors and tactics, but very quickly acquire new sub-actors, new goals and new types of resources and behaviours. In Northern Ireland and in the Middle East, the protest movements broke down into many factions as new leaders came to the fore with slightly different emphases. Thus conflicts that commence as a clear confrontation between one authority and an opposition become complicated with many parties and issues that make the process of resolution all the more difficult.

How can breakthroughs be achieved? What can conflict and peace research contribute?

The Richardson thesis (1960) and the normative perspectives attached to it by Norman Alcock of the Canadian Peace Research Institute (1972), namely that war is a function of the availability of large stockpiles of arms in the hands of selfish and sometimes unstable leaders, who are bound to use them simply because they are there, is too simplistic. Certainly, the quantity and sophistication of arms have a lot to do with the maintenance and severity of conflicts, especially in south-east Asia and the Middle East, and if the world could find a way to reduce the availability of arms, then nation-states might be able to do something about the perpetuation and spiralling of violent conflict. It is more likely, however, that the level of arms can be reduced only when they are no longer felt to be needed. The problems of perceived threat and of conflict have to be resolved first.

In the Third World, war and poverty combine to demoralize entire populations and reduce their capacity to search actively for conflict resolution. War and poverty, which are dramatically obvious to the observer and the main cause of human physical suffering, are but symptoms of underlying structural conditions. The notion of protracted social conflicts provide a deeper insight into the issues of conflict — motivations of those involved, authority roles, political and social structures, behaviour patterns, needs and interests, and other aspects. It draws our attention away from the obvious and the superficial toward the underlying conditions that create conflict situations. It directs our attention, finally, to the means of resolution.

It follows from the above that conflict resolution requires a face-to-face exploration into the needs of the opposing parties and the ways and means of satisfying them. This analytical step appears to be the first and most essential in the resolution of protracted conflicts. Legal frameworks and negotiations over interests are useful efforts if they follow the analytical identification of needs and need-satisfaction mechanisms. Bargaining over interests should not be mistaken for the analytical phase of need identification.

What has become clear is the need for structural change as

part of the process of conflict resolution. One of the most devastating predicaments in the world today is the simultaneous occurrence of conflict and underdevelopment. These two processes feed on each other and make it difficult for societies to overcome either condition alone. In protracted conflict situations, trying to resolve conflict without dealing with underdevelopment is futile. The two have to go together.

Reducing overt conflict requires reduction in levels of underdevelopment. Groups which seek to satisfy their identity and security needs through conflict are in effect seeking change in the structure of their society. Conflict resolution can truly occur and last if satisfactory amelioration of underdevelopment occurs as well. Studying protracted conflict leads one to conclude that peace is development in the broadest sense of the term.

BIBLIOGRAPHY

Alcock, Norman (1972) *War Disease.* Oakville, Ont.: CPRI Press.

Azar, E. Edward (1972) 'Making and measuring the international event as a unit of analysis', *Sage Professional Papers in International Studies,* 1.

Azar, E. Edward (1984) 'Lebanon and its political culture: conflict and integration in Lebanon', chapter 2 in Azar, Edward *et al.* (eds.) *The Emergence of a New Lebanon: Fantasy or Reality?* New York: Praeger Publishers.

Burton, John (1984) *Global Conflict: The Domestic Sources of International Crisis.* Brighton: Wheatsheaf; College Park, Maryland: Center for International Development.

Richardson, Lewis (1960) *Statistics of Deadly Quarrels.* California: Boxwood Press.

Singer, David (1961) 'The level of analysis problem in international relations', chapter 5 in Knorr, Klaus and Verba, Sidney (eds.) *The International System: Theoretical Essays.* Princeton, NJ: Princeton University Press, pp. 77–92.

Waltz, Kenneth (1959) *Man, State and War.* New York: Columbia University Press.

3 The History of International Conflict Resolution

John W. Burton

CURRENT CONFUSION

In the research and applied areas of international conflict resolution this is a period of transition from one main thrust to another: from power bargaining and negotiation to analysis and the discovery of agreed options. It is, understandably, also a time of some confusion over concepts and terminology.

While more and more universities wish to offer courses and to undertake research in the field, and while some governments, including Canada and Australia, are making funds available specifically for this purpose, there is no clear consensus as to approach and content. Definitions of the field of conflict resolution range from deterrent strategies and star wars, through power-bargaining techniques, normative and legal approaches, to psychological attempts to change attitudes of participants in simulation groups to something vaguely termed 'problem solving', which itself can be interpreted to mean any of the above. When the focus is on peace making as distinct from peace keeping, it tends to be on some particular economic, psychological or other aspect of this complex a-disciplinary subject.

Alternatively the focus is on process, as though all that need be known is how to manage a meeting between conflicting parties. There are profitable enterprises that train persons in the art of mediating discussions.

However, it is not just bringing parties together that is important. What is important is the creative input of facilitators. For this reason they must have a wide knowledge of research in the many fields that may be relevant in any particular situation. The third party has a crucial role to play in the discovery by parties to a dispute of options that meet their needs.

In determining which approach to conflict resolution might be adopted in teaching, in research or in practice, there is a comfortable liberal attitude which is to encourage all flowers to bloom. However, some may be weeds with quite poisonous consequences. Conflict resolution as a subject deals with interventions in relations between states and peoples. There are ethical considerations that require professionalism of a high order, and in particular an adequate theoretical framework on which to base tested processes. Some of the above approaches could well do more harm than good. The issues at stake — including protracted local conflicts that spill over into the global thermonuclear system — are too great for such a tolerant approach. Conflict resolution, intervention in relations between nations and states, cannot be based on trial and error, hit and miss or some ideology. It is a serious professional undertaking, in which those concerned may not hide behind the cloak of the 'art of the possible' as diplomacy does. There has to be a high level of prediction and certainty associated with the intervention.

One approach to this intellectual problem is to look at the history of conflict resolution, its varied approaches and the trends that have emerged as a result of experience.

THE LAW AND ORDER MODEL

Let us go back to 1945 when the Charter of the United Nations was drafted at San Francisco. At that time, conventional wisdom held that the global society should be a centralized federal system. The central authority was to have final power to preserve peace. There were certain international legal norms to be observed. There was to be a court to interpret and to apply these. There was to be, also, a body, the Security Council, with enforcement powers. Member states were to contribute forces for the purpose.

The world society was, in short, to be constructed and administered along the lines of the single nation-state. Law and order, majority rule, the common good, were among the conceptual notions that made up the political philosophy of the time.

PHILOSOPHICAL FAILURE

What was not brought to the surface was that this philosophy was a power philosophy: the common good turned out to be, both at the domestic level and at the international level, the common good as interpreted by the powerful. In so far as there was recognition that this was the case, by theorists such as Morgenthau (1948) and by decision makers of powerful states, the belief was that power and the enforcement of power norms could give a stability that was in the common interest.

We now know from experience that even at the domestic level the model on which the UN was based is falsely conceived. It posits legitimate authorities, that is, authorities recognized by the international society by dint of their effective control within their territories. It assumes, however, that these legal authorities are politically legitimized authorities, that is, authorities that derive their legitimacy from those over whom they exercise authority. In the absence of legitimization of this kind, the maintenance of law and order through the coercion of a central authority is a source of violence and protracted conflict.

There are few authorities in the world society that can claim such legitimization. There are some sixty or so domestic conflict situations at present. The use of military forces, internal and foreign, to maintain unpopular governments is widespread. The legal norms of societies are not, in the contemporary world, necessarily those which advance the development of their members. Notions of majority rule generally take little account of the reality of ethnicity and human needs for distributive justice. Dealing with conflicts by the employment of non-legitimized force is not conflict resolution.

The UN was flawed from the outset in two ways. Many of its original members were and are non-legitimized authorities and, as such, the source of serious domestic conflicts that spill over into the international system and invite external interventions by great powers. However, they had and have the protection of a domestic jurisdiction clause that prevents the UN from dealing with their conflicts. The result is a global society plagued with sixty or so serious conflicts at any one time with no institutions that can intervene in any way. It is not an overstatement to say that the UN is a body that affords mutual recognition for many state authorities that lack domestic legitimization. These attract great power support for fear that their domestic conflicts will result in altered ideological affiliations. These are the authorities that are at the source of international conflict.

Even more serious, the UN is flawed by its own non-legitimacy. It has no jurisdiction over matters of international concern that invoke a veto. It has no jurisdiction over matters of domestic concern. In the remaining area — if there is a remaining area — in which it is supposed to have a coercive power through the Security Council, it has no forces at its disposal, as was originally intended. This is, perhaps, all to the good — for its use of force would be only to uphold power norms and, in the longer term, would be self-defeating.

The question we pose is, why is this? It is fortunate that the Security Council has effectively no enforcement powers at its disposal. But why is it that the UN has had no effective role outside a limited peace-keeping role? Why is it that the UN, and regional bodies such as the Organization of American States and Organization of African Unity, make so little impact in the resolution of conflict in cases in which they do have jurisdiction?

DISCOVERY IN INDUSTRIAL RELATIONS

The answer to this question is to be found in the history of conflict resolution. It is hard to believe now, but at the time the Charter was drafted in 1945, few people, perhaps none at San Francisco (including the author who was a member of a delegation), had any clear ideas on the handling of conflict situations outside the traditional law-and-order and power framework. The domestic central authority coercive model was what was in the minds of all as the ideal for an international institution. The goal was to prevent aggression of the German, Italian and Japanese type. Few were educated to ask why this aggression had occurred, what were the background circumstances, and were there problems that could have been solved? In any event, these were not questions to be asked when war with one of these 'aggressors' was still going on.

It was not until the early 1960s that there was any effective challenge to the normative and authoritarian approach of classical theory. When it came, it came in the field of industrial relations. Scholars and consultants such as Blake, Shepard and Mouton (1964) pointed to the need for interaction between management and workers if there were to be cooperation and increased productivity. This coincided with work in decision-making theory in which, for example, Deutsch (1963) focused attention on the advantages of cybernetic or steering and reactive processes, rather than on unadulterated power and hierarchical approaches to decision making.

Once there had been a break from the authoritarian model of decision making and a recognition of the conservation of power that was possible through applying cybernetic processes, it was a short step to interactive models of decision making. In this mode decisions are taken, not as a result of feedback from affected parties, but as a result of poor interaction between them, making feedback less necessary and a relatively inefficient way to proceed.

As in other fields of discovery, there was an exponential rate of development. After a slow take-off, there was an explosion of thought and practice in all fields of behavioural relationships. We are familiar with developments from family counselling to the handling of juveniles by courts. At a meeting of the National Conference on Peacemaking and Conflict Resolution held in St Louis in September 1984, there were five hundred people, young and old, talking the same language of 'problem solving'. They were exchanging experiences of an interactive process, at different system levels. This reflects a significant shift in the theory and practice of decision making and in conflict resolution.

LAG TIME AT THE INTERNATIONAL LEVEL

At the international level there has been little change. The original philosophical framework persists. Man is aggressive, therefore the state is aggressive, therefore national defence is the main priority of state policy, therefore superiority of power is the goal of states — which leads to adversary diplomacy and politics, and to arms escalation. States, and the UN as the institution of states, and the Secretariat of the UN in particular, still see the global society in the classical framework: their approach is normative, relying on mediation or third-party determinations, with an almost total absence of any problem-solving endeavour, in the sense this term is employed in other fields. The Secretary General in an annual report made it clear that change was vital; but it seems that the change he sought was to make the decision-making and coercive nature of the UN more effective by making the Security Council a more effective body (1983). There was no suggestion of alternatives to the traditional mediation process. This was amply demonstrated in 1984 when the Secretary General took an initiative in the twenty-year-old Cyprus dispute. He attempted to mediate within the old bargaining negotiating framework, and, furthermore, made a proposal that assumed acceptance of traditional notions of majority government and power sharing, which contemporary theory and practice have shown to be false.

A SHIFT IN THINKING

At the non-official level there have been some experiments that have arisen out of a quite different philosophy. There has been a paradigm shift of a major order, perhaps too dramatic in that its pace has been too quick for politicians and practitioners, who are usually not in a position to follow theory developments, to absorb. Let us examine this shift.

A group of lawyers in Britain associated with the David Davis Memorial Institute (1966) published their considered view that the institutions available to states were adequate, that is, judicial settlement, mediation, conciliation, negotiation and the other means contemplated within the UN Charter and within classical legal philosophy. They came to the conclusion that there was only one trouble, and that was an unwillingness on the part of states to use the instruments available. This was the conventional wisdom of the time. If only people and nations were law abiding and rational, the existing institutions would be adequate.

The academic community was sharply divided between those who adopted a traditional or power view, and those who adopted what was then termed the 'behavioural' view (not to be confused with the 'behavioural' or quantitative school of the 1960s). The latter sought to determine, not how to settle conflict by the application of legal norms, but the nature of conflict and how to resolve it by an understanding of it by the parties concerned.

SOME EXPERIMENTS

One outcome of this quite bitter conflict of the late 1960s was an attempt by a London group, The Centre for the Analysis of Conflict, to falsify the proposition that disputing parties were unwilling to cooperate in resolving conflicts. Their hypothesis was that parties to disputes would endeavour to resolve their conflicts if they were placed in an exploratory and analytical framework in which they remained free decision makers until an acceptable option was agreed upon, rather than hand over decision making to a court or a mediator.

Obviously some new process would be required, some analytical process that would avoid power bargaining from stated positions and would be exploratory once the goals and objectives of all sides had been revealed. Clearly, this would require an appropriate third party, preferably a panel of four or five scholars who could inject interdisciplinary knowledge and information, not about the conflict at issue, but about conflicts and human behaviour generally.

The test case concerned a conflict in south-east Asia, involving Indonesia, Malaysia and Singapore, which the British Prime Minister of the day, Harold Wilson, had tried unsuccessfully to mediate. With his knowledge and consent the three governments concerned were invited to send nominees to meet in this analytical and exploratory framework at the Centre for the Analysis of Conflict at University College, London. They responded immediately. They met for ten days in a face-to-face situation controlled by a panel of five scholars. The agenda was an analysis of the situation, with no preliminary proposals. There was no bargaining or negotiation. Some unexpected discoveries were made. Whether connected or not it is impossible to say; but fighting stopped shortly afterwards.

This exercise was followed by others which again falsified the proposition that conflicting parties would not meet together. One, Cyprus, was a case being handled by the UN. The UN mediator, Ralph Bunche, had not been able to bring the parties together in a face-to-face situation. Persons nominated personally by the leaders of the two communities concerned, the President (Greek-Cypriot) and the Vice-President (Turkish-Cypriot) met in London within ten days of an invitation being issued. The participants included some who had refused to meet in the official framework. Despite requests from some of the participants, however, there could be no follow-up once the UN again became active.

The same processes were tested at the industrial level and at the community level, in particular in Northern Ireland, until the British government abolished the Community Relations Commission through which they were being carried out.

THE DEVELOPMENT OF THEORY

Falsifying a proposition does not automatically lead to an alternative one. A theory of behaviour had to be developed which would not merely explain why parties were unwilling to meet within existing institutions, but would indicate what kind of institutions would be acceptable and helpful.

This proved not to be possible until there had been further developments by sociologists and others in the general field of conflict and behaviour. Such is the nature of theory building and discovery in the behavioural sciences: it is essentially a-disciplinary. The theory of needs, building on Maslow and others, but stressing values that could not be curbed, socialized or negotiated, as had been assumed was the case, was a creation to which many contributed.

Important among these was Paul Sites (1973). It was he who placed power in a realistic perspective by attributing effective power, not to governments, but to individuals and groups of individuals, who would use all means at their disposal to pursue certain human needs, subject only to constraints they imposed on themselves in their need to maintain valued relationships. He made no reference to international relations as such; but he directed the attention of those concerned with inter-state relations to an important phenomenon. There are certain societal needs that *will* be pursued regardless of consequences. Parties in violent conflict who, for reasons of history and their own behaviour, have no valued relationships, are unrestrained in their use of violence when seeking to pursue such needs.

The next major development came when Azar made a clear distinction between human needs, such as those listed by Sites, which are an ontological part of the human organism, and interests, such as commercial and role interests (1979). Azar's concern at the time was primarily with specific identity-driven conflicts, primarily Lebanon and the set of Arab-Israeli ones. It led him to seek the explanation of what he termed 'protracted social conflicts'. He saw in these the denial both of identity and other such human needs, and of distributive justice, both of which are associated with underdevelopment. Azar was quick to realize that what had first appeared to be a unique situation of ethnic or cultural conflict was but one case of what is practically universal where protracted conflict exists. He developed a general theory to explain why conflicts protract. Ethnicity is clearly an important factor when it is present — which is not unusual — but protracted conflict also relates to underdevelopment, to class conflict, and any problem which involves both identity and distributive justice.

A richer meaning was thus given to the earlier concept of structural violence associated with the name of Galtung (1980). Inevitably there has now developed a renewed interest in political structures that enable the full development of the individual and of the identity group to which the individual belongs. Indeed, the major role of panels associated with conflict resolution seminars is to be innovative in translating the shared values that are discovered into political structures and institutions that will promote their fulfilment. These include decentralized systems and forms of functional co-operation that avoid power and power sharing, thus making possible both respect for identity and effective cooperation between different cultural groups. Structures that are decentralized and rely on functional cooperation rather than élite power are the logical extension of the trends that are part of social evolution, the progressive movement from authoritative power control by a small élite, of which feudalism was a part, to forms of power sharing, to non-power forms of cooperative decision making.

THE PROBLEM OF TESTING

There is one other strand in the history of conflict resolution that should be noted. We are here dealing with what must be regarded as the most complex field of study that man will ever come across: the behavioural relations of humans as persons and as groups. There are no controlled experiments possible. We are dealing with behaviour in open systems. Any control or simulation is likely to lead to false conclusions. We are also dealing with situations in which there cannot be experiments or tests in the ordinary sense. It is not possible, or at least not desirable, to test whether the Soviet or the US is aggressive, or whether NATO and Warsaw deter such aggression, by removing these so-called deterrents. The ordinary controlled experiments or scientific processes do not apply. They are too simplistic for such complex realities.

It happened that, during this period of development of behavioural theory, the philosophy of science was also developing. What was previously described as scientific method was found to be not so scientific, and indeed useful and reliable only in limited circumstances. The debate between Kuhn (1962) and Popper (1957) revealed some shortcomings in controlled experiments and in empirically based theorizing. It also demonstrated that a formal deductive approach that relied upon falsification was impractical, as such testing was usually not possible in open systems.

A third possibility emerged with the greater interest in Peirce's early work on 'abduction' (1980) in which, unlike that of Popper, a scientific value was attached to the validity of the original hypothesis. This led to a questioning of the consensus assumptions of traditional political theory. Empirical work was directed toward observations that previously were not made. It was apparent, once the observer was alerted to question assumptions, that the traditional concepts of law and order, of the common good, of majority decision making, of the right to rule and to expect obedience, were probably at the root of a great deal of conflict. Clearly this was the case in situations where there was an absence of political legitimization. The attempt to impose structures that denied to people their identity and their development in all aspects, and the attempt to impose the norms of the powerful, were dysfunctional and a source of conflict.

RECENT DEVELOPMENTS: INTERESTS AND NEEDS

We now come to the present day and the work of the Center for International Development at Maryland where it was felt that parties to disputes required a process that would allow them to make a meaningful analysis of their relationships in a face-to-face situation, even though they did not 'recognize' each other or might be in a state of war.

The theory of needs led logically to this development of a process that would enable parties to conflicts to ascertain the hidden data of their motivations and intentions, and to explore means by which human–societal needs held in common could be satisfied. As these needs were universal, and as they related to security, identity and other developmental requirements that are not in short supply, the process soon revealed that conflict resolution with win–win outcomes is possible. The Center was able to test both theory and process in actual situations.

The theory and process, as stated originally by the London group, had a Utopian ring. It seemed to ignore the political and material realities of conflicts and their protracted nature, despite all manner of attempts to manage them.

It was for this reason that a differentiation between needs and interests, that is, between values that are not negotiable and interests that can be traded, was a major one in practice as well as in theory. Classical thinking led us to believe that conflict was about interests only. For that reason it was thought that the individual could be socialized and coerced. What both theory and application revealed was that protracted conflicts, which are the major concern in world politics, are primarily over non-negotiable values. They are concerned with human and identity needs such as those listed by Sites. This being the case, it is impossible to socialize the individual over any length of time into behaviours that run counter to the pursuit of security, identity and other aspects of development.

This is a significant development, not just because it clarifies the role of conflict resolution, and overcomes the ring of Utopianism. It also removes a major source of the confusion in the area of conflict resolution to which reference was made at the outset. There are those who are concerned with improving bargaining and negotiation techniques. There are those who are concerned with problem-solving techniques. They have been and are still somewhat at loggerheads. Now it is clear that there are situations in which negotiation of the traditional type, and even normative processes, are relevant in some circumstances. There are other circumstances in which these traditional means of settling disputes are not relevant and which require problem-solving techniques.

In due course we will be clearer about which are which and where there is a merging of the one into the other, as, for example, when cultural identity is defined in terms of political control. In the meantime, the warning flag is out: conflicts such as wage disputes, and conflicts over unattractive islands in the South Atlantic, may not really be over negotiable interests. They may relate to values that are not for trading. Indeed, it may well be that conflicts are protracted unnecessarily just because inalienable values are translated into interests merely to fit into the traditional processes of bargaining and negotiation. If there were other processes available, the hidden data would be revealed and could be dealt with.

FURTHER TESTING

Within this more sophisticated theoretical framework, the Center for International Development has been able to tackle two interesting conflict situations: Falklands/Malvinas and Lebanon. Already two facilitated face-to-face meetings have taken place in each case. In the first the participants have been members of the relevant committees of the two legislatures. In the second they were the nominees of leaders of the different communities.

SETTLEMENT PROCESSES AS A CAUSE OF PROTRACTED CONFLICT

There is one other observation that should be made. It seems likely that the traditional processes of power bargaining and mediation are themselves an additional reason for conflicts to be protracted. It is they which lead to temporary settlements without tackling the underlying issues.

Related to this are the dangers associated with peace-keeping forces. In the absence of parallel analytical and facilitated processes of conflict resolution, peace keeping tends to institutionalize conflict, to make it part of the way of life, making any resolution all the more difficult.

There will be many further insights, giving rise to innovations in theory and practice. However, we are at last justified in assuming that the knowledge level in conflict resolution is now such that there are no substantial ethical reasons for not moving ahead. Perhaps the most important task ahead is training and communication of what is now known. There is a great burden of traditional thinking to be removed.

THE PROBLEM OF CHANGE

At this time we can offer some hope to a world society that seems devoid of it. But it is restricted hope. The evolution of civilizations has required change and adjustment to change, yet survival of the fittest requires built-in mechanisms for preservation against change until existing structures can no longer meet the challenge of competing ones. Leadership and élites seek to conserve existing roles and institutions by whatever power means are at their disposal until overcome by more powerful forces. Societies have always been in conflict because some sections of them have drives for change stemming from their pursuit of their human needs, while others fear it and its threat to their interests. Change having been regarded as malign and antisocial, we have not developed even a language of change, except a malign one — revolt, revolution, dissent, terrorism. Without a language and a conceptual framework we could have no theory of change, and, therefore, no processes of change, except those of power and violence. The conflict resolution processes that have now evolved are effective only to the extent that parties to disputes are helped to cost accurately the consequences of change or no change. In this sense the processes of facilitated conflict resolution are designed to cut down the delays that occur in change, and to speed up the evolutionary process toward greater fulfilment of societal needs.

Within these limitations it can be claimed that we are moving towards insights and processes in which bargaining of needs against interests can be avoided, and in which the parties concerned can define needs and interests and cost the consequences of preserving interests at the expense of needs. It is, furthermore, a process, unlike change by organized violence, to enable parties to move from point A to point B conscious of the outcomes. In this way change can be more than merely the substitution of one ruling élite for another which will also pursue sectional interests at the expense of human needs.

Translated on to the global scene and the relations between the great powers, this is a significant discovery. Both sides fear change lest it prejudice their relative power positions. Yet both sides know that change in very many political systems is not merely inevitable, but also desirable. The US does not particularly desire to defend repressive feudal systems in Central America and elsewhere throughout the globe; but it fears the consequences of unpredictable political change. The Soviet Union, if we can deduce its position from reactions by scholars there, was astonished and dismayed by the high level of violence that followed change in Ethiopia. If there were a means of reliably bringing about change with desired outcomes, many situations in the world society would no longer attract great power interventions.

These considerations direct attention to what is probably the most serious problem in global politics, for it constantly leads the great powers into conflict: the deformities of domestic systems. These deformities are not confined to smaller and underdeveloped states. The US has its share and they make it most defensive against the introduction of more egalitarian systems anywhere in its sphere of influence. The Soviet Union is self-conscious of its non-participatory society and becomes anxious when there are demands in bordering states for increased participation, even if only at the work level.

One dreams of an institutionalized means by which conflict situations are subjected to problem-solving processes before there is any transfer of arms or any interventions by the great powers or by others. The dream includes each of the great powers giving the other the opportunity to change, rather than attempting to exploit the existence of deformities that will finally lead the one or the other to some desperate act of survival.

Perhaps the elusive great power summit meeting should focus, not on arms control (a futile exercise until there is a lessened felt need for arms), but on the employment of processes and techniques that are now available, thanks to years of scholarship in many fields of inquiry. It is in this direction that the UN must go if it is not to be regarded as an irrelevant body in the field of conflict resolution.

BIBLIOGRAPHY

Azar, Edward E. (1979) 'Peace amidst development'. *International Interactions,* **6**, No.2.

Blake, P.R., Shepard, H.A. and Mouton, J.S. (1964) *Managing Inter-Group Conflict in Industry.* Houston: Gulf Publishing Co.

David Davis Memorial Institute, (1966) *Report of a Study Group On Peaceful Settlement of International Disputes,* London.

Deutsch, Karl (1963) *The Nerves of Government.* New York: The Free Press.

Galtung, Johan (1980) Articles in *Journal of Conflict Resolution,* and 'A structural theory of imperialism: ten years later' in *Millenium,* **9**, 3.

Kuhn, Thomas (1962) *The Structure of Scientific Revolutions.* Chicago: University of Chicago Press.

Morgenthau, Hans (1948) *Politics Among Nations: The Struggle For Power and Peace.* New York: Knopf.

Peirce, C.S. (1980) in Levi, I. 'Induction in Peirce', in Mellor, D.H. (ed.) *Science, Belief and Behavior.* Cambridge: Cambridge University Press.

Popper, Karl (1957) *The Poverty of Historicism.* New York: Routledge & Kegan Paul.

Sites, Paul (1973) *Control, the Basis of Social Order.* New York: Dunellen Publishers.

4 Psychology of the Self in Social Conflict

Bryant Wedge

Social conflicts at any level regularly display certain common features. Prominent among these are polarization into we–they identification, predictable perceptual distortions, proliferation of conflict issues and, frequently, escalation spirals. These observable features reflect roots in the psychology of the individuals who belong to the social unit. They greatly complicate the processes that arise from a struggle over immediate interests that are usually presumed to be the basis of conflict; they also complicate the process of conflict resolution.

If elements of the psychology of individuals enter into social conflict, it follows that conflicts arouse psychological responses in the members of groups. In fact it is demonstrable that some behaviour of normal persons who are involved in group conflict would be defined as insane under any other conditions. The question arises, then, what is the link mechanism between individual psychology and group conflict? How is the character of social conflict affected by the psychology of social memberships? A consequent question is, how can the psychological nature of conflicts be taken into account in managing conflict?

Let me begin with a common observation: members of groups involved in serious conflict with other groups display very high levels of emotionality, especially hate-filled rage with destructive intent. Such feelings are not merely social behaviour demanded by group opinion, but are intensely personal. Indeed, in conditions of civic disorder or warfare they are expressed in extraordinarily murderous or suicidal behaviour.

There is exquisite sensitivity to slight or to boundary incursion. Hurt feelings occur from experiences of the group that are very far removed from any effect on the person.

All of these phenomena are familiar to the psychologist. They are typical of the defence of the integrity of the personal self, of self-esteem. It is clear that members of groups (especially ethnic groups) and nations respond to threat or injury to the group as a whole exactly as they would to narcissistic injury, hurt to the self. Eric Fromm observed that individuals responding to group insult 'are as sensitive as the individual narcissist, and they react with rage to any wound, real or imaginary, inflicted upon their group ...' (1972). Such reactions of group members aggregated into mass behaviour provide a powerful driving force toward conflict, a force divorced from the ostensible struggle over interest.

In the individual the powerful dynamism of response emerges, first of all, from encounters with others. Initially this response is a favourable regard of infant caretakers. Inevitably, disappointment ensues as the child learns limitations to the admiring recognition it seeks. Attempts at compensation, through primitive grandiosity and paranoid projection, represent distinct phases in the attempt to secure self-esteem at almost any price. While these are usually passing phases, the capacity to regress to such 'solutions' remains.

As we will see, grandiose and paranoid solutions may occur on a mass basis when social groups to which individuals have become committed suffer humiliation. Given this response, certain 'irrational' aspects of group behaviour become understandable. The motive of self-esteem is a powerful force: individual responses constitute the unit of behavioural analysis.

Except in pathological cases, the childish solution is superseded by a further effort to gain self-regard — identification with other and more powerful objects in an expanding sequence: parents, family, local figures, landscapes, culture heroes, the flag, the ethnic group and the nation. Identification leads to incorporation of these social objects into the self-system. We have called this the extended self of the person. Identification depicts the relationships schematically: it indicates the continuity between the individual and his/her social investments (Figure 4.1) (Wedge, 1978).

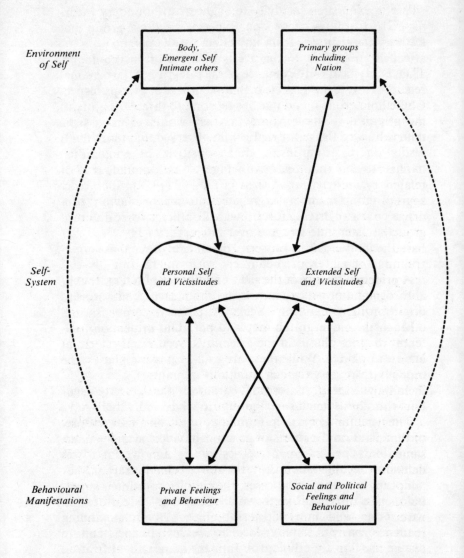

*Figure 4.1: Schematization of principal self-system links
between individual and social behaviour*

We are now in a position to outline some of the implications of individual self-involvement in the conflicts of groups. Reference to the schematization illustrates how social events affecting the part of the self that is extended to the group may arouse personal responses. Conversely, highly individual reactions may be experienced and acted on in the social sphere. Consequently group members, reacting personally to slight, insult, humiliation or alienation by the group, respond with defensive hypersensitivity or narcissistic rage reactions (Kohut, 1972).

This highly emotional quality of response can in no way be related to actual issues in contest. It is when they are aggregated that they lead to wholly irrational behavioural drives, not explicable in rational man as a model for inter-group or international behaviour in conflicts. These feeling-based responses, unless recognized and accommodated, contribute to the interactive escalation of disputes.

A principal quality of the self — and hence of self-system — is the quest for recognition. It will be remembered that the origin of the personal self depends on recognition by the other — 'the gleam in the mother's eye'. This remains consistent throughout life. More or less subtle demands are made on others to acknowledge one's being. The non-recognition of individuals is the source of their endless and relentless anger, including murders committed on others who are important, but who fail to accord recognition.

The need for recognition is solidly rooted in the psychology of the self. Translated into its manifestation of social self, the same dynamic response is elicited. Groups and nations demand that their unique existence be acknowledged. They adopt varieties of symbols and exhibitions representing their uniqueness and requiring attention. Denial of recognition or narcissistic disacknowledgement appears to stimulate rageful reactions; many of the sources of political terrorism appear to rest on this dynamic. When the Prime Minister of one country stated, reflecting a hope, that another people never existed, several thousand of those negated volunteered as terrorists within a week. These were the rage-filled acts of individuals.

Similarly, the problems of juridical recognition become fraught with overtones of self-reactivity and elicit levels of emotion far greater than the actual issues would seem to merit. Hence questions of sovereignty are much more difficult to resolve in so far as they are experienced as involving betrayal of the integrity of the self. Non-recognition as a diplomatic statement, then, may have much more serious consequences than are intended and sometimes lead to intractable conflicts.

In managing conflicts in which recognition demands have become prominent, there is no possibility of negotiation. Recognition is difficult to define as an interest. However, this intangible need of the human person is so valuable that the mere granting of acknowledgement can often bring disproportionate dividends in a negotiation process. Once symbolically acknowledged, negotiation partners become more flexible on 'real' interests. In fact, it appears that one of the meliorative effects of third parties in conflict management is the capacity of the third party to accord recognition to the disputants while they are unwilling to offer it to each other directly.

Another dynamic quality of the self is its need to sustain cohesion and a sense of wholeness. As has been mentioned, this leads to the incorporation of inanimate objects in the extended self, such as the landscape and other symbols. Hence, violation of boundaries or assaults on group property, no matter how worthless the bit of territory or how minor the loss of property may be, arouses real and personal fear of fragmentation so that the reaction is disproportionate to the cause. Many a battle has been fought over a bit of land that no one really wanted. And, in major cases of religious sites, a jealous possessiveness may prevent any rational compromise. These are not interests in any economic sense, they are needs of the heart and in the end serve the need of the integrity of the self of social members.

It is impossible to negotiate over absolutes, but we may note here that these items which are treated as absolutes are, in fact, symbolic. Recognizing this shifts the level of discourse for it is sometimes possible to satisfy symbolic needs with symbolic concessions; permitting flags to fly, ceding titular sovereignty or paying token compensation for damages may restore a sense of wholeness and reduce the level of conflict. The trouble here is the interactive nature of conflict which prevents the perpetuating agent from admitting fault. Once again the third party acting with careful tact is sometimes able to move the dispute to a problem-solving stance.

The phenomena of narcissistic rage are precipitated by various forms of humiliation based on a sense of unfairness or injustice. Defeat in a fair competition is accepted by the prideful self; it is when one is forced to accept unequal rules and finds oneself helpless and unable to gain acceptance that this type of rage ensues. It is characterized by the relentless pursuit of the destruction of the offending humiliator. Unlike other sorts of inchoate rage, this sort of reaction is characterized by the use of intelligence and patience in pursuit of the goal.

When narcissistic rage is aroused by humiliation of the group, the search for revenge, and fighting what is perceived as a wrong, becomes evident from the reckless disregard for the humanity of others, for the rules of normal competition or even for the enraged person's own life. The angry narcissist is able to carry out complex plans for revenge, whether they be the small plots of terrorist assassination or complex state policies. France Fanon's *Wretched of the Earth* (1963) speaks to this dynamic and has been read with approval by dispossessed peoples in much of the world. He argues that only through violence can dignity be regained.

The management of narcissistic rage is extremely problematic. It requires that offended persons be given every opportunity publicly to assert their identity and to explain their complaint. This runs flatly counter to the normal impulse to isolate and show up such unrestrained actors. Yet, in a dozen cases in the world today that policy is obviously failing. We must call this an unsolved, but quite serious problem. Incidentally, the prescription above is based on management of particular cases, and does not imply necessarily a need to yield to demands, but to hear them and acknowledge them.

What is argued here is that the self-system of individuals provides a powerful linkage with the behaviour of groups in social conflict. Non-rational human needs, including those especially for recognition and 'justice', provide a driving force in conflict behaviour and need to be taken into greater account in conflict analysis than is commonly the case. Moreover, management of conflicts absolutely requires accommodation of the needs of the individual members of social groups for continuity and integrity of the social self. Conflict is always especially psychological. Problem solving must take this into account.

BIBLIOGRAPHY

Fanon, F. (1963) *The Wretched of the Earth*. New York: Grove Press.

Fromm, E. (1972) *The Anatomy of Human Destructiveness*. New York: Holt, Rinehart and Winston.

Kohut, H. (1972) *Thoughts on Narcissism and Narcissistic Rage: The Psychoanalytic Study of the Child*. New York: Quadrangle Books.

Wedge, Bryant (1978) 'The self system and group violence', *American Journal of Psychoanalysis*, **38**, pp. 111-20.

5 Conflict and Collective Identity: Class, *Ethnie* and Nation

Anthony D. Smith

Human history has always been witness to two kinds of conflict. The first has been universally regarded as 'normal', the competition between states or any duly constituted political authorities. From the first clashes between rival Sumerian city-states in the third millenium BC to the set-piece battles of eighteenth-century European dynastic states, warfare between polities has punctuated the historical record and marked the 'waxing and waning' of political power. From time to time, however, we read of another kind of conflict, wars between whole peoples and classes. Such popular uprisings often took the form of peasant jacqueries or religious rebellions. Sometimes, groups of city-states raised the standard of revolt against alien empires, like the Ionian cities against the Persian empire in 499 BC or the Swiss valley cantons in AD 1291 against their Habsburg governors (Andrewes, 1971, p. 65; Thurer, 1970, pp. 25-6). Though we tend to treat such popular conflicts as unusual, perhaps 'abnormal', they were far more common than we had imagined, even in premodern times. Today, the popular type of conflict is the most protracted and bitter; for not only does it involve more fundamental passions than inter-state wars, it is also much more frequently intertwined with the rivalries between states, so that the two kinds of conflict now flow together to produce increasingly dangerous conflagrations. Under modern conditions, popular antagonisms of class and ethnicity that had often been latent and frozen have today become acute and manifest political issues, and new antagonisms created by their example and by

63

modern social conditions are constantly being added to the repertoire of contemporary conflicts.

'INSTRUMENTALISM' AND COLLECTIVE IDENTITY

Reading the diplomatic and political histories of the nineteenth and early twentieth centuries, one could be forgiven for concluding that war and conflict were the prerogatives of states and their ruling élites. Even today, there is a widespread feeling, popular and academic, that state interests and the imperatives of the system of states, economic as well as political, furnish both the causes and the issues for most wars. That is very much the standpoint, not just of governments, but of the international agencies that seek inter-state cooperation. Not only does this assumption accord with their perceived interests, it also makes sense of their ideal of systemic stability and orderly progress towards global economic development. It is in terms of 'states' and their populations that multinationals invest and market their products, and international agencies plan their programmes of aid. And it is for these selfsame 'nation-states' that governments and international agencies alike make educational, welfare and security provisions.

Unfortunately, this standpoint and its 'statist' assumption glosses over a fundamental problem. This is that very few of these states, which constitute the unit of world order today, are in fact genuine 'nation-states'. Walker Connor has shown that just 10 per cent of the member states of the United Nations could in 1972 make that claim, and some 50 per cent were seriously divided along ethnic lines (Connor, 1972). No wonder that politicians, statesmen and international bureaucrats regard nationalism as a force *sui generis*, to be grappled with as best they can, like some inexplicable disease or millennial religion (Kedourie, 1971, Introduction). To the guardians of the inter-state order, nationalism seems like the Black Death, striking discord wherever it appears and gripping the collective psyche of the 'masses' to overturn perfectly coherent and rational political arrangements, and even threatening old-established, democratic European states.

Now, as long as we continue to adopt this 'statist' view of international politics and disregard the structural location of factors like class, ethnicity and nationalism, we shall preclude all understanding of these powerful phenomena and render ourselves unable to deal with their political consequences. The fact is that the 'statist' view of world history with its skewed emphasis upon the inter-state system, the 'balance of power' and a world divided into political units and regional economic zones, grossly underestimates the potency of certain kinds of identity and community, and systematically fails to address the roots of successive conflicts 'on the ground'. It is certainly important to locate local and regional conflicts within the wider structure of superpower blocs and their client-systems that undergird the inter-state order, and to see how the latter can manipulate grass-roots conflicts for their own ends. But 'fishing in troubled waters' requires latent local antagonisms and their prior politicization to be effective. The first question then is to ask why these local conflicts assume so bitter and chronic a character and why so many human beings are prepared to sacrifice their lives and inflict violence on each other for causes that from afar seem insignificant — or amenable to rational, peaceful resolution. In other words, our contemporary political analysis must focus on the second (socio-economic and socio-cultural) level of conflict and the ways in which it habitually spills over into the regular rivalries between states (Seton-Watson, 1978; Smith, 1979, ch. 8).

Why then is it that large numbers of people are mobilized for conflict and war, and why is this occurring with such frequency in the modern world, when one would have thought that the fires of nationalism were extinguished?

The answer given by one school of modern theorists is that, in a world of scarce resources but high communication, individuals find it useful and necessary to form collective units for the pursuit of wealth, power and prestige; élites and individual leaders in their competition with other leaderships for power and resources need to mobilize followers for success; and bases like class or ethnicity afford convenient 'sites' for mobilization and coordination of interests of different sections of the population. For writers like Daniel Bell, Paul Brass and Cynthia Enloe (Enloe, 1973 and 1980; Brass, 1974 and 1979;

Bell, 1975) ethnicity, in particular, is fundamentally 'instrumental'. It combines economic interests with cultural 'affect' and is, therefore, often superior to class in its ability to provide a base for mobilizing people in support of collective policies or the pursuit of power. This standpoint owes much to the researches of the social anthropologist Frederik Barth (Barth, 1969). In his profound study of premodern ethnicity, John Armstrong uses Barth's notion of ethnic community as a bundle of shifting interactions with outsiders and boundary mechanisms between 'them' and 'us' to analyse the changing and often overlapping boundaries of religion, class and ethnicity among medieval Christian and Muslim communities (Armstrong, 1982).

A second 'instrumentalist' school of theorists proceeds from the economic dimensions of ethnicity and nationalism. They argue that modern capitalism and industrialization have brought formerly isolated ethnic communities together by increasing social intercourse between people. As a result, the more favoured 'core' states (Britain, France, etc.) were able to exploit their initial advantage in both having a strong state and an early market capitalism (Wallerstein, 1974). After 1800, their bourgeoisies were able to impose an economic (and later political) imperialism on many countries of Asia and Africa, which led to resistance by the peripheral élites who were forced to appeal to 'their masses' to counter the political threat contained in this uneven expansion of capitalism (Nairn, 1977, ch. 2, 9). Even within their own boundaries, these 'core' states exploited their peripheral hinterlands and communities, so that today, Scots and Welsh, Basques and Bretons, Corsicans and Catalans are reaffirming their identities in the face of this economic exploitation and cultural discrimination (Hechter, 1975; Hechter and Levi, 1979; Stone, 1979).

Yet a third 'functionalist' standpoint proceeds from the needs for communication in modern capitalist or industrial societies. Using Karl Deutsch's communications approach, albeit in quite different ways, recent theorists like Ernest Gellner and Benedict Anderson focus on the uses of language and education in creating identities today (Deutsch, 1966). For Gellner, premodern agro-literate societies had no room for nations or nationalism, since they were necessarily culturally divided along class lines. But today modern industrial societies require a mobile and trained population to run their complex social machine. Modernization uproots people and throws them together in the anonymous city, where their only bond is language and formal education. This kind of public, standardized, mass education requires larger nation-states to sustain it and hold people together, now that their traditional role relations have been eroded. Unfortunately, certain culture traits like religion and colour refuse to be blurred by mobility and assimilation. At this point, two nationalisms emerge and two new nations are formed (Gellner, 1964, ch. 7.; Gellner, 1983). For Anderson, the ever-present need to surmount death which the old religions had tried to assuage, and the new possibilities opened up by the technology of 'print-capitalism' with its flood of books and magazines, have made it both necessary and possible to imagine communities which are both sovereign and limited, that is, 'nations'. Thus, the need to overcome death by linking oneself to a community of destiny and posterity, and the opportunities of new modes of communications, furnish the bases for a sense of identity with anonymous individuals who are in specified ways 'like us' and who inhabit the same homogeneous calendrical time (Anderson, 1983).

All these approaches and theories certainly take the problems of class, ethnic and national identities seriously and remind us of their intrinsic importance in the modern world. But they still underplay the explosive power of such loyalties. It is not easy to see why so many people should die, or kill each other, for small pieces of territory or the right to influence state policies or run their own affairs, if classes, ethnic communities and nations are just so many 'sites' for mass mobilization or neglected peripheral communities or clusters of culturally similar populations mobilized by uneven development. All these approaches reveal the 'class' dimensions of many an ethnic conflict and are perhaps better suited to the explanation of intra-state or international class divisions. And yet, class antagonisms are probably the most amenable of the three types of community and identity to peaceful conflict resolution, involving as they do economic interests more than basic identity needs and fears. It is the other, ethnic and national, conflicts that have proved most difficult to surmount or alleviate. Hence, in what follows, it is these which I have mostly in mind.

'PRIMORDIALISM' AND THE ETHNIC REVIVAL

A quite different, albeit minority, school of theorists holds that ethnic identity is primordial and perennial and that nations are the natural unit of history and an integral part of the human equipment. If we leave aside the more sociobiological versions of this idea, which argue that ethnicity is a product of partisan groups organizing for survival through kinship ties (van den Berghe, 1978), we are left with the view that language, religion, race and territory provide the basic organizing principles of human existence throughout history, and that these 'primordial ties' of humanity have always divided the species into culture-communities, as naturally as have sex or geography (Geertz, 1963; Fishman, 1972 and 1980; Connor, 1978).

This view has much to commend it historically. The record is full of named culture-communities divided along religious, linguistic, ethnic and territorial lines. From time to time, these communities formed the basis of ethnic states such as ancient Egypt or Sassanid Persia and when such *ethnie* became directly involved in the habitual warfare of states, there is little doubt that the ensuing fighting was more envenomed and drawn out. One has only to think of the long and bitter wars of Romans and Carthaginians, or the resistance of the Jews of Palestine to Roman imperial power, or that of the Swiss against the Habsburgs, (Smith, 1981b). And when class alignments are superimposed upon religio-ethnic ones, as in the Tai P'ing rebellion in mid-nineteenth-century China, the struggle becomes even more deep-rooted and widespread (Wright, 1957; Bellah, 1965; Wolf, 1973).

Nevertheless, the 'primordialist' standpoint overstates the case. The fact that ethnic ties and sentiments fluctuate greatly in their salience and effects in different periods and areas, suggests that a simple theory which posits the universality and naturalness of ethnicity cannot account for important empirical variations. It may be that language, religion and territory, together with kinship, are as old as *homo sapiens* (perhaps older, if we think of Neanderthal 'religion'); but ethnic communities (*ethnie*) in the sense of named human populations with shared myths of descent, historical memories, culture, a territorial association and a sense of group solidarity, are a later development, which first comes to light in the record in the later third millennium BC, (Moscati, 1962; Kramer, 1963; Brass, 1979).

Certainly from this point onwards, ethnicity has played a role in history that we ignore at our peril, but the social importance of *ethnie* at any one time or place has varied considerably, and it is sometimes difficult to pinpoint the shape, duration, intensity and social penetration of ethnic ties and sentiments in premodern eras (Smith, 1981a, ch. 4). More germane still, premodern *ethnie* were rarely politicized: that is, they rarely became the focus and subject of political action and political community.

But this is just what has occurred in the modern world. Instead of 'withering away', as most modernization theorists expected, ethnic and national ties have experienced something of a revival, while new *ethnie* have been formed in unlikely places. Why has this occurred, and what does it bode for our planet?

The ethnic revival has happened in our times for a number of reasons. The first is the growth of an intelligentsia. Because of the decline of traditional religion and the priesthoods that were its guardians, and because of the rise of rationalism and science, a new stratum of intelligentsia has emerged to take the place left by the diminishing priesthoods. The process is by no means complete. There are significant areas, particularly in Islamic lands, where the clergy retain much influence and can initiate a backlash against the professional intelligentsia and their rationalism, using those same sentiments of identity and dignity that the intelligentsia themselves make use of. One has only to think of the Shi'ite revival in Iran and beyond (Halliday, 1979; Keddie, 1981). Nevertheless, the new intelligentsia themselves, often thwarted in their quest for prestige and power in the newly rationalized professions and bureaucracy, are ready and able to lead the masses in their perennial revolts against constituted authorities of the state. They are drawn towards the historical vision of the intellectuals with their belief in the destiny of separate nations, because such visions offer professional people new hope for worthy employment of their talents and training, (Seton-Watson, 1960; Smith, 1981a, ch. 6).

A second reason for the ethnic revival, which has moved in successive waves across the world since the French revolution, has come from the impact of the modern, rational or 'scientific' state on society. The pressure exerted by this form of polity for standardization and homogeneity has meant the uprooting of traditional and customary ways of life, and a profound practical challenge to older religious conceptions of the world. Ethnic communities in polyethnic states are now drawn into the political mêlée. Urbanization, mass education and conscription, all under the aegis of the rationalized state, both dislocate their old folkways and disrupt their beliefs. At the same time, they offer new opportunities in a secular world, yet severely curtail them in the interests of a levelling and homogenizing state. But the 'state' is nearly always an 'ethnic state': that is to say, it is nearly always dominated by a larger, strategic *ethnie* (there are exceptions like Nigeria and Yugoslavia), and was originally built up around that 'ethnic core'. Hence state homogenization always appears to the nondominant *ethnie* like ethnic discrimination and exploitation. In an age of nationalism, that perception is likely to prove explosive (see Olorunsula, 1972 for some African examples of nationalism in polyethnic states).

Third, there is the impact of nationalist ideology itself. The aspiration for a 'nation' is not the same as that for ethnic survival. For the 'nation' is something more that the *ethnie*: it involves the idea of equal legal rights for members (the basis of citizenship), it requires a common division of labour or economic unity, and it entails a mass, public, compulsory, standardized education system which will endow all the citizens with a common political culture or civic religion (Smith, 1971, ch. 7; Weber, 1976; Gellner, 1983). These were the ideals of civic or 'territorial' nationalism as it first arose at the time of the French revolution. Subsequently, ethnic components were added to the territorial ideal of the nation: a common myth of descent, shared historical memories and group solidarity. New states striving to create 'nations' found they had to include these elements, particularly in the artificially formed 'state-nations' of Africa (Rotberg, 1967; Smith, 1983a). In this they looked back to the experience of Eastern European nationalisms with their already formed *ethnie* seeking separate states of their own, which would confer on them the qualities of territorial nations (Sugar and Lederer, 1969). In the end, nationalist ideology became a powerful mixture of ethnic and territorial elements, with, at its root, a directive myth of origins and descent which embodied the burning sense of thwarted and oppressed identity obscurely felt by so many members of unrecognized *ethnie*.

Fourth, there was the inter-state system itself. This had, after all, come into being after the Treaty of Westphalia in Europe in 1648, and subsequent treaties had simply expanded it, both in space and in substance (Tilly, 1975). This meant that in Europe, and later outside, the inter-state system was in place *before* the onset of nationalist ideology in the early nineteenth century. Hence, newly revived *ethnie* and aspiring nations were 'knocking at the door' of an already constituted state system, to which they sought a ticket of admission. And, inevitably, one day, there was felt by the powers-that-be to be no more room, no social and geopolitical space left for new would-be nations. The ensuing resistance to new claimants by the constituted 'nation-states' only mirrors the inner identity feelings of the *ethnie* and would-be nations themselves, just as, in another sphere, the exclusion by the upper class or bourgeoisie of lower classes simply mirrors their sense of historic alienation. Hence, the more they suffer exclusion, the more this inflames their sense of thwarted identity and the more they desire collective (ethnic or class) self-determination. (Ronen, 1979; Smith, 1983b).

The generic result of these internal and external conditions and pressures is a renewal of the sense of identity and dignity among human populations who feel (and often are) excluded from the centres of power and from a legitimate 'home' and recognized 'roots' in the order of societies. It is these conditions which fuel and mobilize the sentiments which inform the myth of descent. The myth of origins and descent, in turn, is the most conspicuous and unique element in that complex of myths, memories, values and symbols which mark off *ethnie* and nations and around which such distinctive collectivities have been crystallized. For these myths summarize and unfold powerful ties of belonging and sentiments of collective dignity and self-respect, through which multitudes of otherwise rootless and homeless and fragmented individuals can find a worthy historical location and destiny. Though there are also myths of *class* origin, it is the ethnic and national varieties that, especially today, give form and purpose to the most fundamental ties and passionate sentiments underlying popular mobilization. Herein lie the basic values of heroic worth, ancestral reverence, familial passion and self-renewal, and the pride of antique pedigree and unique memory which the heedless onslaught of modern technology and onrush of modern social development alike threaten to engulf and submerge (Smith, 1984a).

In this myth are stored many of the most sacred and valued memories and sentiments of individuals and families. For it explains to them:

> (1)   their origins in time and space: when they originated, whence they came, thus setting out barriers, temporal and spatial, to the flood of meaninglessness that otherwise might sweep them away;
>
> (2)   their ancestry and descent: who first begat them, and how they are related to, and descended from, their presumed ancestor, even where he/she is largely mythical, as with Abraham or Oguz Khan among the Jews or Turks;
>
> (3)   their migrations and liberations: how they wandered to their present habitat, how the land became 'theirs' and how they were freed from oppression;
>
> (4)   their golden ages: how they became great and glorious, how they produced mighty heroes and sages, how their genius flourished in its own land;
>
> (5)   their present sad decline: how they lost their inner moral fibre, how they declined from their former glory, how they became oppressed or exiled, in a state of weary decay;
>
> (6)   their future rebirth: how they will soon be reborn, and

how they must strive for self-renewal and be regenerated in their own land and under their own laws and rule.

Undoubtedly, the point of the 'myth' lies in this last summons to mobilize the people for political action. It is a nationalist mythology built on the political and cultural premises of nationalism. Though it draws on much older myth-motifs current among earlier generations of the community and handed down in oral traditions or epics and chronicles, the elaborated mythology of many present-day communities is the work of nationalistic intellectuals who have delved into the history, philology and anthropology of their communities and have tailored the broadly evolutionist model of social history to their own ethnic ends (Smith, 1984b). It embodies the values of these intellectuals and their followers among the professionals, for whom personal dignity and identity are closely bound up with the political fortunes of their community of origin. Ethnic myths of descent have become their charters of rights.

IDENTITY CONFLICTS AND THE INTER-STATE ORDER

What do these grass-roots developments mean for the pattern of politics across the globe? Clearly, they are not conducive to a peaceful and orderly development of inter-state relations or to stability and harmony within states. Nor does it help to try and 'explain away' the disruptions and endemic passions unleashed by ethnic and national myths of identity and dignity by suggesting that purely economic solutions can be found which will compensate for, or divert from, the basic lack of recognition of identity needs and fears. Economic solutions are not wholly irrelevant, wherever class alignments are superimposed upon more fundamental ethnic or national cleavages. In Lebanon, for example, it is possible to alleviate some of the Christian–Muslim tensions by manipulating the property system and distribution of wealth in favour of the underprivileged Shi'a and Druse communities. But this will never come to grips with the underlying distrust or meet the basic identity and security fears and needs of the various communities in Lebanon — Maronite, Druse, Shi'a and others.

The fact that, in Lebanon and elsewhere, class divisions have quite often become superimposed upon ethnic or national alignments, because of uneven development or core–periphery relations or élite ethnic competition for scarce resources, as suggested by the 'instrumentalists', simply adds another dimension of grievance and alienation to an already embittered situation. Quite often, we find that unacknowledged ethnic or national communities are *also* economically underprivileged and exploited. At the same time, the fact that we find nationalizing among 'overdeveloped' *ethnie* in regions with higher living standards than the political 'core' or majority community in the state, such as the Catalans and Basques in Spain, or the Slovenes and Croats in Yugoslavia, suggests that economic disparity, although often an important additional factor, does not furnish the root cause or figure among the underlying conditions of explosive ethnic nationalism (Connor, 1977; Smith, 1979, ch. 6).

It is rather to the sense of exclusion and failure in the social and political world, created by the modern state and by nationalism, that we should look for the root causes and underlying conditions. As we have seen, what they amount to is a systematic denial of the aspirations of particular *ethnie* and would-be nations for social and political recognition, and an inability to make provision for the respective security fears and identity needs of various communities. If the sense of identity and dignity of individuals has become increasingly focused on the *political* rights of the communities into which they have been born, or have opted to join, then any international order that seeks to minimize injustice and conflict must address itself to their *political* aspirations as communities. Unfortunately, the present rigidities in the inter-state order, the lack of mechanism for further recognition and incorporation of *ethnie* (apart from ex-colonies), together with the general reluctance to grasp the nettle of *collective*, as opposed to individual, rights and identities, when it is *collective* rather than individual identities that at present move people most and produce the greatest violence, prevent international organizations, governments, regional associations and other bureaucratic agencies from coming to grips with the real problems that engender conflict today.

For one only has to consult one's geopolitical map to realize that the most chronic and insoluble conflicts are those that involve political claims for recognition and accommodation of collective identities, especially those of ethnicity and nationality. In Ulster, the basic cleavage is ethnic and national. Though class dimensions have been superimposed, with the Catholics relatively underprivileged and property-less, the historic conflict has been centred on myths of descent founded on rival, mutually exclusive readings of religio-communal history. These in turn stem from the superimposed cleavages which, starting with geopolitics and religion, divided an embittered Irish peasantry and later middle class from a Protestant Anglo-Irish gentry and their English overlords (Lyons, 1979). In Cyprus, the conflict is plainly ethnonational. Not only does it involve a confrontation of ethnic communities, with their separate religions and life-styles, not only did British colonial policies help to create further divisions in the period of post-war crisis, but the broader, historical conflict of Orthodox Greek and Muslim Turk, though abated somewhat by Ataturk's policies and a forced exchange of populations on a massive scale, has remained a constant and a baseline from which violent excursions could be periodically launched (Campbell and Sherrard, 1968; Kitromilides and Couloumbis, 1976). In the Middle East, too, the Arab–Israeli dispute that has lasted over thirty-five years and five wars again revolves around a case of dual recognition of group identities and rival territorial–ethnic myths, the one Jewish and Israeli, the other Arab and Palestinian. No solution which does not encompass their mutual fears and needs for security and recognition is likely to prove lasting or fruitful (Avineri, 1976).

In the heart of Europe, in Berlin, the tensions are usually portrayed in global East–West terms. But it is no less clear that the ambiguities of two Germanies, the sense of burden over a divided *ethnie* and its recent destructive past, are likely to prove the deeper cause of any upsurge of violence beyond immediate economic issues, just as one element in the Polish crisis is the sense of national frustration in the working out of the Polish communal destiny. In other parts of the world, too, group self-determination and myths of identity have generated violence and conflict. In the Indian subcontinent, we have seen violence over rival claims to Kashmir by India and Pakistan, each regarding the territory as part of their historic heritage, and over the recent claims of Sikhs to greater autonomy, even a separate state of their own, in which to practise their faith and restore their sense of identity and destiny. In the south, too, in Sri Lanka, riots between Tamils and the majority Sinhalese over their respective rights and communal dignities threaten to spill over into Tamil-populated India (Brass, 1974; Seton-Watson, 1977, ch. 7).

It would be quite easy to multiply such examples in south-east Asia, the Middle East, Black Africa and, in a milder form, even in Western Europe and North America (Quebec, etc.) (Said and Simmons, 1976). Enough has been said, however, to underline the contemporary prevalence and destructive potential of ethnic and national conflicts, often abetted by class inequalities and based upon a widespread sense of thwarted identity and unacknowledged dignity, which is guided and fuelled by underlying inner myths of descent.

Because of the rigidities and power interests within the inter-state order, group identities are likely to be frustrated and thrown into internecine conflicts. Neither the bureaucrats of the international agencies and governments nor the executives of the multinationals are in any position or frame of mind to accommodate and recognize the claims of embattled *ethnie* and would-be nations. As a result, the fire behind identity sentiments bent on restoring and regenerating their communities in accordance with their 'myth of descent' spends itself in vain on the iron grid of the inter-state order and, turning back in its tracks, falls upon neighbours and rivals, threatening to engulf whole regions in bloody wars. Nor are the superpowers above manipulating such rivalries and conflicts, if they can. Thus local conflicts come to mirror those within the inter-state order as a whole, with *ethnie* compelled to align themselves along a capitalist versus communist axis which is quite foreign to their particularistic aspirations (Richmond, 1983).

There is a further consequence of this international failure. Because superpowers, multinationals, medium states and international agencies accord recognition only to states and not to *ethnie* or other communities, they are generally willing to condone, or at any rate acquiesce in, the authoritarian measures used by most states to contain ethnic and class dissidence. Whether it be Franco or Pinochet, Karmal or Kenyatta, there is a general reluctance to thwart, or even criticize, the repressive measures undertaken to quell class or ethnic discontent, exactly because of the 'sanctity' of the state as the sole political norm. This means that the inter-state order is, more or less directly, involved in sustaining in power often brutal regimes and turning a blind eye to their institutionalized violence. State violence, however, only evokes further terrorist violence, with the result that nobody can break the cycle initiated by unrecognized communal claims, or distinguish between the 'reasonable' or 'unreasonable' elements contained in them. Where ultimate power interests are felt to be at stake, and where on the other side ultimate identity needs are engaged, there can, in the present structure of international (read: inter-state) society, be no compromise and no hope of a peaceful solution (Wilkinson, 1974).

INTER-NATIONALISM AND INTER-COMMUNALISM

This is a bleak picture, and the prospects, in the short term, are worse. As far as the political eye can see, the 'international community' has neither the vision nor the tools to extricate itself from the prospect of further spirals of violence between states and communities. By its refusal to separate 'state' from 'nation', the way out is blocked. Enabled to see only fully fledged 'nation-states', and those imperfectly, the inter-state order and its ruling apparatchiks cannot unfreeze the existing status quo of 'admitted states', unless it be to *replace* an existing member-state with a claimant (e.g. Israel by Palestine, Taiwan by China). As a result, the inter-state order is blind to changing power centres which are built on communal identities and their regenerative myths, and therefore is powerless to intervene in 'cycles of violence' as they erupt in region after region. The net result is untold misery for innocent people caught up in the fighting, surges of refugees, massacres and revenge killings, sterner governmental repression, and ultimately the danger of superpower involvement and confrontation.

If the above analysis is correct, then it would follow that we must radically change our focus and entrenched positions, if in the long term we are to move towards a saner and less brutal world. To begin with, the 'international community' must move away from a wholly statist analysis to one which is more communally centred. It must break the arid and blind vision of a world of bureaucratic states, to which all other potentially political entities must conform or perish. This means, for example, that it is no good forcing statist solutions on to communally divided areas like Ulster, Cyprus or Lebanon. Nor will it help to propose solutions that do not take the respective communities' identity needs and anxieties into account, such as forcing Catholics in Northern Ireland to submerge their identity in a Protestant-Ulster state, or vice versa.

What, then, can be done? Here it is necessary to look at some of the detailed work of recent conflict resolution theory, as spelled out in subsequent chapters. As far as the problem of collective identity is concerned, what is required is patient, sensitive analysis and approaches which identify problem areas and then attempt to deal with each in turn. This involves paying as much attention to cultural and psychological needs and anxieties as to economic or political interests. Indeed, in the case of ethnic identities, the cultural–psychological factors are pivotal. No amount of economic improvement devoid of political recognition and cultural understanding can hope to defuse tense and bitter ethnic cleavages; if anything, the opportunities and expectations opened up by economic development will enhance the sense of frustrated collective identity and thwarted political recognition. This has been amply demonstrated in Lebanon, Flanders, Quebec, Palestine and Croatia, where conditions have improved for the politically unrecognized or underprivileged minority (sometimes a numerical majority in the state) (see Esman, 1977; Hall, 1979; Stone, 1979).

It may be objected that an 'inter-communalist' approach which re-focused our vision on to communities rather than states could open the floodgates to universal group self-determination and thereby increase the potential for conflict ten- or one hundred-fold, particularly in Asia and Africa. Certainly, this is what many a Third World leadership fears, and for good reason, given the state interests which form their power base (Neuberger, 1976; Markovitz, 1977; Saul, 1979). Their quite genuine fears might indeed be realized, if the international community and organizations were to prefer the claims of each community in its dispute with the state, or if such community orientation would produce a mirror international image of conflicts between communities. But this would be simply to replace one extreme by another, with its attendant ills. What is needed is the patient and sensitive examination of each claim in its *context*; and that context will include the claims of both rival communities and the interest of incorporating states. For example, the claims of the Kurds have to be set in the context of their diaspora across five contiguous states, each with their own interests and communities, and the ensuing problems of granting Kurds a measure of unity and autonomy. But this is quite different from the current international disregard of a Kurdish problem, in the hope that the sentiments of a thwarted Kurdish identity and community which have received only partial recognition in Iraq will somehow evaporate (Edmonds, 1971).

To solve this and other identity conflicts, the international community must examine simultaneously the social conditions and the cultural–psychological fears and needs. This means inducing a situation in which new inter-communal as well as inter-state ties are forged, not opposing the needs of communities to each other or to the interests of states. New ties and interests would have the effect of peeling away the layers of superimposed cleavages which harden conflicts and of disaggregating interests that have become unduly clustered together. Lines of cleavage would no longer be sharply dichotomized; instead they would cross-cut each other, producing more varied interests and needs. As far as the cultural–psychological dimensions are concerned, a number of strategies and methods are needed. These include the isolation of specific issues and the scaling of the priorities of each community's needs and fears; finding 'compensations' for any losses that settlements might entail; including the communities in wider regional groupings which would be supportive of their security needs; de-linking, as far as possible, communities' needs and fears from complicating outside interests and communal ties of a 'Pan' nature; educating new generations of the community to respect the collective dignity and needs of other communities, even so-called 'enemy' ones; and repartitions to defuse the most troublesome demographic nodes of violence.

Of course, some of these measures can only be considered as a last resort, since it is, in the last analysis, individuals and families whose rights the international community ought ultimately to protect. The fact remains, however, that for the reasons outlined earlier, most individuals and families today identify their individual rights with collective ethnic, class and national identities based on the historic charter of myths of descent and fired by sentiments of thwarted dignity. For this reason, none of the above strategies and methods of alleviating communal conflicts can have any validity or utility unless they form part of a new vision of international politics, a vision that places communities of historic identity nearer the centre of its concern, which seeks to provide an international mechanism for recognizing strong and durable collective identities wherever they present themselves with their passions and their myths, and which accords their claims for a collective status in the modern world order a measure of genuine expression. Ultimately, this entails finding ways of including stable and durable communities whose aspirations have been curtailed within the international community, either through states of their own or through national status within federations. For it is only through such collective recognition and inclusion that we can hope to move towards a less brutal, more just and more stable world.

BIBLIOGRAPHY

Anderson, B. (1983) *Imagined Communities*. London: Verso Editions and New Left Books.

Andrewes, A. (1971) *Greek Society*. Harmondsworth: Penguin.

Armstrong, J. (1982) *Nations before Nationalism*. Chapel Hill: University of North Carolina Press.

Avineri, S. (1976) 'Political and social aspects of Israeli and Arab nationalism', in Kamenka, E. (ed.) *Nationalism, the Nature and Evolution of an Idea*. London: Edward Arnold.

Barth, F. (1969) *Ethnic Groups and Boundaries*. Boston: Little, Brown & Co.

Bell, D. (1975) 'Ethnicity and social change', in Glazer, N. and Moynihan, D. (eds.) *Ethnicity, Theory and Experience*. Cambridge, Mass.: Harvard University Press.

Bellah, R. (1965) *Religion and Progress in Modern Asia*. New York: Free Press.

Brass, P. (1974) *Language, Religion and Politics in North India*. London: Cambridge University Press.

Brass, P. (1979) 'Elite groups, symbol manipulation and ethnic identity among the Muslims of South Asia', in Taylor, D. and Yapp, M. (eds.) *Political Identity in South Asia*. London: SOAS, Curzon Press.

Campbell, J. and Sherrard, P. (1968) *Modern Greece*. London: Benn.

Connor, W. (1972) 'Nation-building or nation-destroying?', in *World Politics*, **XXIV**, pp. 319-55.

Connor, W. (1977) 'Ethnonationalism in the First World', in Esman, M. (ed.) (1977) *Ethnic Conflict in the Western World*, Ithaca: Cornell University Press.

Connor, W. (1978) 'A nation is a nation, is a state, is an ethnic group, is a ...'. *Ethnic and Racial Studies*, **I**, pp. 377-400.

Deutsch, K. (1966) *Nationalism and Social Communication*, 2nd ed. New York: MIT Press.

Edmonds, C. (1971) 'Kurdish nationalism', *Journal of Contemporary History*, **6**, pp. 87-107.

Enloe, C. (1973) *Ethnic Conflict and Political Development*. Boston: Little, Brown & Co.

Enloe, C. (1980) *Ethnic Soldiers*. Harmondsworth: Penguin.

Esman, M. (ed.) (1977) *Ethnic Conflict in the Western World*. Ithaca: Cornell University Press.

Fishman, J. (1972) *Language and Nationalism*. Rowley, Mass: Newbury House.

Fishman, J. (1980) 'Social theory and ethnography', in Sugar, P. (ed.) *Ethnic Diversity and Conflict in Eastern Europe*. Santa Barbara: ABC-Clio.

Geertz, C. (1963) 'The integrative revolution', in Geertz, C. (ed.) *Old Societies and New States*. New York: Free Press.

Gellner, E. (1964) *Thought and Change*. London: Weidenfeld & Nicolson.

Gellner, E. (1973) 'Scale and nation'. *Philosophy of Social Sciences*, No. 3, pp. 1-17.

Gellner, E. (1983) *Nations and Nationalism*. Oxford: Basil Blackwell.

Hall, R. (Ed.) (1979) *Ethnic Autonomy – Comparative Dynamics*. Oxford: Pergamon.

Halliday, F. (1979) *Iran: Dictatorship and Development*. Harmondsworth: Penguin.

Hechter, M. (1975) *Internal Colonialism*. London: Routledge and Kegan Paul.

Hechter, M. and Levi, M. (1979) 'The comparative analysis of ethno-regional movements', *Ethnic and Racial Studies*, 2, pp. 260-74.

Keddie, N. (1981) *Roots of Revolution*. New Haven, Conn.: Yale University Press.

Kedourie, E. (ed.) (1971) *Nationalism in Asia and Africa*. London: Weidenfeld & Nicolson.

Kitromilides, P.M. and Couloumbis, T.A. (1976) 'Ethnic conflict in a strategic area; the case of Cyprus', in Said, A. and Simmons, L. (eds.) *Ethnicity in an International Context*. New Brunswick: Transaction Books.

Kramer, S.N. (1963) *The Sumerians*. Chicago: Chicago University Press.

Lyons, F.S. (1979) *Culture and Anarchy in Modern Ireland, 1890–1939*. London: Oxford University Press.

Markovitz, I.L. (1977) *Power and Class in Africa*. Englewood Cliffs: Prentice-Hall.

Moscati, S. (1962) *The Face of the Ancient Orient*. New York: Books.

Nairn, T. (1977) *The Break-up of Britain*. London: New Left Books.

Neuberger, B. (1976) 'The African concept of Balkanisation', *Journal of Modern African Studies*, XIII, pp. 523-9.

Olorunsola, V. (ed.) (1972) *The Politics of Cultural Subnationalism in Africa*. New York: Anchor Books.

Richmond, A. (1983) 'Ethnic nationalism and post-industrialism', *Ethnic and Racial Studies*, 7, pp. 4–18.

Ronen, D. (1979) *The Quest for Self-Determination*. New Haven: Yale University Press.

Rotberg, R. (1967) 'African nationalism: concept or confusion?', *Journal of Modern African Studies*, IV, pp. 33–46.

Said, A. and Simmons, L. (eds.) (1976) *Ethnicity in an International Context*. New Brunswick: Transaction Books.

Saul, J. (1979) *The State and Revolution in East Africa*. London: Heinemann.

Seton-Watson, H. (1960) *Neither War, Nor Peace*. London: Methuen.

Seton-Watson, H. (1977) *Nations and States*. London: Methuen.

Seton-Watson, H. (1978) *The Imperialist Revolutionaries*. Stanford: Hoover Institution Press.

Smith, A.D. (1971) *Theories of Nationalism*. London: Duckworth; New York: Harper and Row. Second Edn. Duckworth and Holmes and Meier, (1983).

Smith, A.D. (1979) *Nationalism in the Twentieth Century*, Oxford and New York: Martin Robertson and New York University Press.

Smith, A.D. (1981a) *The Ethnic Revival*. Cambridge and New York: Cambridge University Press.

Smith, A.D. (1981b) 'War and ethnicity', *Ethnic and Racial Studies*, 4, pp. 375–97.

Smith, A.D. (1983a) *State and Nation in the Third World*. Brighton: Harvester Press.

Smith, A.D. (1983b) 'Ethnic identity and world order', *Millenium*, 12, pp. 149–61.

Smith, A.D. (1984a) 'Ethnic myths and ethnic revivals', *European Journal of Sociology*, 25, pp. 283-305.

Smith, A.D. (1984b) 'National identity and myths of ethnic descent', *Research in Social Movements, Conflict and Social Change*, 7, pp. 95–130.

Stone, J. (ed.) (1979), 'Internal colonialism', *Ethnic and Racial Studies*, 2.

Sugar, P. and Lederer, I. (eds.) (1969) *Nationalism in Eastern Europe*. Seattle: University of Washington.

Thurer, G. (1970) *Free and Swiss*. London: Oswald Wolff.

Tilly, C. (ed.) (1975) *The Formation of National States in Western Europe*. Princeton: Princeton University Press.

Van den Berghe, P. (1978) 'Race and ethnicity: a sociological perspective', *Ethnic and Racial Studies*, I, pp. 401–11.

Wallerstein, I. (1974) *The Modern World System*. New York: Academic Press.

Weber, E. (1976) *Peasants into Frenchmen: The Modernisation of Rural France, 1870-1914*. London: Chatto and Windus.

Wilkinson, P. (1974) *Political Terrorism*. London: Macmillan.

Wolf, E. (1973) *Peasant Wars of the Twentieth Century*. London: Faber and Faber.

Wright, M. (1957) *The Last Stand of Chinese Conservatism*. Stanford: Stanford University Press.

6 Problem Solving in International Relations

A.J.R. Groom

Problem solving is an approach to disputes that now is widespread in the Anglo-Saxon world. It has grown rapidly in the last twenty years at many levels: the personal level, the industrial level, the inter-communal level, and, indeed, it has also been tried at the international level. There are many techniques, but they all share certain features. They all try to create an unusual non-routine setting in which consideration of the parties' joint problem is possible, rather than a situation in which the prosecution of the conflict by negotiation and bargaining is the main aim. In other words problem solving is a process designed to create a situation in which all parties feel that they have, according to their own criteria, 'won' and not merely have done well in a situation where there are winners and losers.

Problem solving attempts to create a situation in which there is the 'shock of the new', that is, where the parties come to realize that they do not have complete information about the conflict, and especially, that they do not know in sufficient detail or accuracy the objectives and motives of their adversaries. It is a process that helps the parties in a dispute to confront the fact that in some respects their definition of the problem may need to be revised and that they may have misunderstood the perception of other parties about the nature of the dispute.

Parties, in this situation, thus learn about themselves and their relationship with their adversary, from their own behaviour, from their adversary and from a third party. The third party's role is different from that traditionally conceived in, for example, mediation: it is to be supportive of all the parties and not to press compromises.

The problem-solving approach often uses the academic paraphernalia of a seminar in order to achieve its purpose. Seminars do not have fixed agenda; they explore a topic. Discussion without limits, following the thread wherever it leads, is a common opening move. The need to put ideas to the test in an empirical examination of statements is another essential element in the process. There is also the academic tradition of respect for persons and for the view of others.

Moreover, the goal of the exercise ultimately is the *resolution* of a conflict, not a simple settlement. Resolution in this sense means that a new set of relationships will eventually emerge which are self-sustaining and not dependent for their observance upon outside coercion or third parties. It is not a settlement imposed by a victor or a powerful third party, but rather a new set of relationships freely and knowledgeably arrived at by the parties themselves.

Now this is not a panacea. It may not always work. Whether it does or not, is probably more a question of efficiency in operation than of the issues at stake. The goal is to get what the parties want at the least cost, all things and people considered, in the long run. It emphasizes a long-run perspective. It offers an alternative when the parties realize that they are in that gnawing situation of not being able to win even though they cannot be defeated, or of not being able to quit, even though it is costing them a great deal. It does not require goodwill, it does not require peace-if-only-people-were-reasonable. It does not require a conversion of the individual participants. On the contrary, their re-entry problem when they return to their social group requires that they retain their values.

Problem-solving differs from traditional approaches. One traditional approach is to try to arrive at some moral decision on the basis of a consensus. That, of course, is highly successful in minor disputes where there is a broad underlying consensus. When such a consensus is lacking the legal or moral approach is merely a propaganda weapon. An alternative is to move into coercive bargaining or traditional power politics. Here the best outcome is very often an imposed settlement based on continuing and, in the long run, very costly coercion. Problem solving tries to put the relationship in a different framework, aiming at resolution rather than settlement — a resolution which is self-sustaining without coercion. It is based on the idea that parties may have to move, but they do not have to lose. It is likewise based on the idea that all parties — no matter how respectable they are, how strong they are, how deviant they are, how badly they are thought to have behaved in the past — are included in the process. That means in effect that all parties, even those basically capable of sabotaging the process, must be included. It is political realism.

How does this approach fit into the context of the UN Charter? The UN Charter lists many means of peaceful settlement of disputes: negotiation, inquiry, mediation, conciliation, arbitration and judicial settlement. We have some forty-five years of experience of these means in the UN framework. International problem solving builds on this experience in other contexts, such as the industrial. The most usual way of approaching conflicts in the past has been through face-to-face negotiation. But the frequent result of this, in the absence of a neutral element, is that the parties dig themselves into a rut. They revive all their old prejudices and stereotypes about each other. It is all too often, at best, a dialogue of the deaf.

Judicial settlement (and arbitration), on the other hand, is not favoured in most serious conflicts because it is non-participatory, because it is judgemental and because, very frequently, it supports the status quo. Thus those who want change, and those who fear it, are equally unlikely to accept judicial settlement or arbitration. The parties want to retain control of the decision-making process in its entirety, including the outcome, and not to cede it to a judge or to an arbitrator. They want to decide what happens to them, and not leave it to somebody else to decide. Thus increasing recourse is being made to mediation and even more to conciliation because of their participatory and non-judgemental nature.

Parties only trust themselves, but they do need help. The question is what sort of help? It is help with processes, help with information about what happens in conflict and about the perceptions of others. The third party cannot tell the parties to the conflict what the outcome should be, only they can decide that. If there is to be a resolution, it is the parties themselves that must be the potential and ultimate actors.

Problem solving grows out of the tradition of mediation and conciliation. However, it moves further towards analysis and decision by the parties themselves. It suggests a new role for the third party. The third party is not looking for a compromise, it is not trying to give direction, but it is trying to give information of a different sort. Here the conflict researcher, supported by practical experience in other spheres, has developed a number of techniques which can be applied in this framework. For example, it seems highly productive not to give salience in the discussion to history, law, past bad faith, atrocities and the like because usually they can be cited in plenitude but they cannot be changed. Instead it is useful to begin by asking the questions, 'What is the problem?' and 'How can it be resolved?' rather than whether one party or the other is right or wrong and should be judged one way or the other. The task is to define the problem. The third party protects the conflicting parties from the past, from letting the past write the future, and encourages them to think about an acceptable future relationship, putting aside, however hard it may be, the past relationship.

The problem-solving process is extremely useful in breaking down stereotypes. In practically all conflicts at all levels thinking in stereotypes and stereotypical reactions become predominant. One does not think, one reacts. What is more, 'tunnel-vision' is common: people become fixed on one thing and they cannot see what is a little to the left, or a little to the right. The range of options seems very limited. The job of the facilitator — the third party — is to widen that tunnel-vision by pointing out that people act in response to the environment as they see it, as best they can. However violent or objectionable their behaviour appears to be they are very often reacting in ways that others would in similar circumstances. Moreover, the role of the third party is frequently to reveal self-fulfilling prophecies and self-defeating actions, and to point out that if policy is based on a 'worst case' analysis, then parties are likely to effect the worst case. In fact, the worst case is not necessarily the most likely case.

The facilitator also strives to make sure that the parties

differentiate between what their declared policy is and what their action is, so that the other side sees the difference between the two. While it may be necessary to say some things in public for political reasons, this may not mean that this represents what a party is going to do tomorrow, or ever.

It is important for the third party also to help the conflicting parties to break a problem down into manageable components so that, at the end of the day, there will be something, no matter how trivial, on which there can be agreement.

Problem solving is to look for the superordinate goals, that is, goals which both sides individually want but can only get by cooperating together. It is only possible, for example, to have tourism in Cyprus, which both communities want, if the level of conflict is such that bullets are not flying about. That is a superordinate goal. To develop a sequence of such goals is helpful as it brings the parties into a satisfactory relationship based on their own interests as they see them.

Problem solving often involves consideration of decision-making processes. Frequently parties in conflicts assume that the other side acts rationally, that what it does it intended to do and that a whole theory of its behaviour can be built in a coherent logical way. At home, of course, things are not like that at all. At home it is a mess, it is chaos, it is short-term fixing. Things happen which were never intended to happen and decision makers are trapped into a framework from which they would like to escape, but do not know how. Actions frequently have unintended consequences that are deplored, but that cannot be wished away. To help people understand the process of decision making by the different parties is a frequent task of a facilitator. Furthermore, it is important to see how political leaders often get riveted into, and entrapped by, a particular policy which they cannot abandon despite its obvious cost and lack of success. Once good money has been spent on a bad option it is very difficult politically to give up that option.

The process of scuttling often involves the painful change of political leadership. For this reason, political leaders cling, ensnared, to their own policy. Conflict resolution seeks to find ways of enabling them to change. It also needs to find occupations for war leaders when they become peace leaders.

People who are very good at leading conflicts may not be very good, as the British electorate told Winston Churchill, when it comes to leading the peace.

There is a need to think of some unconventional possibilities such as unilateralism, not in the sense of nuclear unilateralism, but in a different sense. Sometimes, if it is believed that there is a possibility of agreement, a unilateral beneficial act by one party for another is required, which is inexplicable in terms of the present level of conflict, but which may change perceptions. That is a very dangerous policy, as President Sadat found out when he went to Jerusalem. Unilaterally, he gave away many good debating points that had been defended with vigour over many years. Prime Minister Begin seemed to carry on as he had before after pocketing the windfall. But unilateralism sometimes works. When the Schumann Plan was proposed, France was in a strong position, it was making major concessions, it was saying to the Germans 'Come on, join with us rather than fight against us', and it got a favourable response. It is a risky policy to be sure, but it is one that could be tried in other contexts. Moreover, the more conventional alternatives, too, are not without their risks.

One of the 'tricks' that a facilitator may try is to persuade the parties to a conflict actually to describe their conflict in a mutually agreed way. They can very rarely do that, but they learn a great deal about themselves and other people's perceptions in trying to do so. It is also important to destroy the notion that one's own conflict is worse, more bitter, more difficult than anybody else's. Parties to conflict often argue that theirs is the worst imaginable, but they cannot all be right. Every conflict, of course, has its unique elements, but it also has common elements. A facilitator can be very useful to the parties by putting their conflict in this perspective of the common pattern and of how other people have felt about and dealt with this or that facet of their conflicts.

The aim of facilitation is to enable the parties to learn about each other, their perceptions, and their actual and potential goals, and to encourage the parties to indulge in a private exploration of their problems, without commitment, or prestige or status being involved. The participants speak 'off the record', personally and for themselves alone, but they are briefed and very often 'blessed' officially by the head of their party. Their first duty, of course, is to tell the facilitators about the inequities of the other parties, albeit usually in polite terms. They have to get it off their chest. The facilitators listen, but the other parties often do not, in the sense that, although they hear the words, they do not perceive what is behind them.

Then the facilitators take over. They talk about conflict in general, about theories and hypotheses, and involve the participants in a theoretical study of other people's conflicts before gradually reverting to their own conflict. There tend to be cycles of euphoria and pessimism, but sometimes there is a learning process, a re-perception, a re-costing, so that gradually the conflict becomes a problem to be resolved rather than a fight to be won. It is important in this process that the participants be hard-liners as well as authoritative, because any re-perception carried home from a problem-solving exercise will carry weight and credibility when stated by a noted 'hawk'.

Such procedures are an innovation at the international level, but private diplomacy of this genre is more widespread and influential than is generally acknowledged. Problem solving responds to a felt need for an alternative and it is an alternative, and not a replacement of traditional channels, since any insights must ultimately be fed back into the normal world of international diplomacy. A need is felt when traditional methods have led to a costly stalemate, but such cases are the most difficult. This suggests that, in the long run, problem-solving procedures should be available in a preventive mode. This aspiration will undoubtedly encounter formidable problems in getting international actors to have recourse to 'preventive medicine'. Yet the assets of the method are attractive — full participation in an exploratory exercise of a confidential nature, involving neither coercion, status nor judgement, moving not towards a distribution of roles and resources on a win-lose–compromise basis, but to a resolution of the conflict without losers. Above all, it has an increasing relevance in a diverse world with a variety of actors in complex interdependence at all levels, with both coercive and cooperative transactions, in which, at the highest level — nuclear relations — if there are any losers there are likely to be no winners.

7 The Procedures of Conflict Resolution

John W. Burton

INTRODUCTION

'Winning' is the aim of all parties engaged in a dispute. In matrimonial, industrial, class, race and international relations disputes, the aim of all is to win. By winning, interests and ambitions are preserved and attained.

'Winning' is, to some extent, an end in itself. Our culture requires us to attach a high value to winning. Games are typically win-lose. Competitive relationships, personal and commercial, are win-lose. Party politics are win-lose. Court procedures are win-lose. We live in adversary institutions and these are, by their nature, win-lose.

When 'winning' is a goal in itself, it can be defeating of other, even more valued, goals. In a party political system, in order to 'win' it is necessary to oppose. Sometimes it is necessary to oppose what one seeks! When 'winning' is a goal it can lead to losing important interests and values. In matrimonial and industrial disputes, the need to 'win' can lead to the loss of the longer-term relationships and goals that are sought by trying to 'win' the conflict!

Whether winning is in relation to interests and aspirations or is a goal in itself, 'winning' has consequences for the loser which lead the loser to behave in ways which destroy the 'gains' of victory. In personal and group relationships, it is possible to win the conflict and as a result lose future relationships. In industrial relations, lasting and costly antagonisms frequently follow 'victory' by one side. In international relations continuing confidence, respect and good faith is a mutual security need, especially among great powers. Yet this is destroyed for generations by one side deliberately 'winning' in some power-bargaining negotiation.

The explanation of this paradox is that there are intangibles in all relationships that ultimately off-set the gains of victory: intangibles such as responses to humiliation, to a sense of insecurity, to a perception of injustice, to a sense of lack of consideration and respect.

So there is a dilemma. Interests, values and needs require winning conflicts, yet winning is dangerous in its consequences.

The dilemma would be avoided if it were possible to arrive at win–solutions, that is, agreements that gave to all parties what they were seeking. This includes their interests and goals and, also, the status and satisfactions from winning for its own sake. Is this seemingly unrealistic outcome possible? In what circumstances and by what means can win–win outcomes be achieved?

Let us pose this question by reference to two simple continua: from power to cooperation and from win–lose (or lose–lose) to win–win.

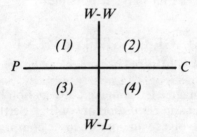

Quadrant *4* in the illustration above depicts something with which we are familiar. It is the quadrant in which would be put games — win–lose, but win–lose according to rules which make the outcome acceptable. Quadrant *1* would accommodate typical paternalistic decisions: the parties are thought to benefit as the result of a decision by some person or institution exercising power. Quadrant *3* is the one with which we are familiar in conflict situations. There is power bargaining or even war, with winners and losers or, perhaps, all losers.

Quadrant *2* is the one in which would be placed conflicts with outcomes in which all parties are winners.

The question we are posing is whether this quadrant *2* represents only an imaginary outcome of conflict, some ideal unlikely to be attained except in the most favourable circumstances, or whether, on the other hand, win–win outcomes of conflict may be generally possible.

This seems, in our culture and in our experience, a curious question. Political relations and our experience suggest strongly that conflicts arise out of objective differences of interest and rivalries over scarce resources. They must be win–lose. It would be a shift in thinking of a profound kind — like finding the earth is round and not flat — if we were to discover that conflicts have generally a win–win potential and not a win–lose one.

And this is what we are suggesting. It is not idealism, not a religious faith, not wishful thinking. It is political and practical realism.

The onus of proof is on those who challenge conventional wisdom. If win–win is possible, what makes it possible? What reasons do we have to suggest that win–win is possible? What are the processes that make it possible?

THE LANGUAGE OF SETTLEMENT AND RESOLUTION

Just for convenience let us make a distinction between *settlement* of conflict and *resolution* of conflict. Settlement is when the outcome involves win–lose or some compromise in which all or some parties are to some degree losers — and probably feel somewhat aggrieved. For example, parties have been obliged to share a scarce resource and cannot be wholly satisfied. Some coercion is probably necessary to enforce the settlement. Resolution is when there is an outcome which fully meets the felt needs and interests of all parties. It is, therefore, self-sustaining. For example, parties have been able to share a resource in plentiful supply and are wholly satisfied. Settlement relates to quadrant *3* and resolution to quadrant *2* in the diagram in the Introduction.

We are familiar with the processes of settlement, the processes by which the proportions of gains and losses are determined. They include *judicial settlements, arbitration, mediation, conciliation* and *direct bargaining.* They reflect the application of legal and social norms or the consequence of relative power. We know how courts, arbitrators, mediators and conciliators work and we know of the various forms mediation takes and the role of the mediator.

The notion of the resolution, however, is strange to us. Conceptually we can comprehend win–win outcomes, but they are not part of our ordinary experience. Indeed, we do not have an appropriate language. The process could well be termed *problem solving.* However, whereas we have a clear image of a court or a bargaining table, we have no such image of a problem-solving institution. For want of a better term, some who experiment with problem solving refer to '*workshop*'. These two terms, problem solving and workshop, are far from satisfactory because they have other meanings in English. Yet they have their merits. Problem solving is a useful term because a problem in relationships remains even after there is a final settlement. It is not until an option is discovered that satisfies the interests and needs of all parties that the problem is solved. Problem solving implies exploration and not merely the simple processes of bargaining. 'Workshop' is similarly useful because it suggests that all the parties concerned have to get down to the analytical job of problem solving. They have to work at it. It may even be time consuming. As is the case with all workshops, there are skills and techniques and tried processes. There is, also, the guidance of an instructor or tutor.

It is useful to confine the term *negotiation* to the final stages of settlement or resolution. Once there has been agreement in principle there remain the tasks of determining details and drafting an agreement. This narrow and more precise meaning of the term separates bargaining from negotiation and problem solving from negotiation, thus making clearer the distinction between bargaining and problem solving.

The bargaining process is often assisted by a *mediator.* This term implies, clearly, a third party whose role it is to suggest a reasonable compromise, an allocation of wins and losses.

Problem solving implies no mediation process in this sense. However, it rests no less on a third party — the instructor or tutor in the workshop. The role is quite different. The term we reserve for the third party in the problem-solving process is *facilitator*.

Parties to disputes have their own definitions of them: they are about wages, territory or some other issue. It is not necessarily the case that the declared issues are the real ones. A wage dispute could be triggered by hostility to management or unclean toilets. An international dispute basically about security could be defined by reference to some territorial claim. In a bargaining, mediation and settlement mode, these declared issues are those on which compromise is sought. In a problem-solving mode it is the issues underlying those that are claimed that have to be discovered and analyzed. For this reason it is useful to distinguish between *tactics* and *goals*. The claim for territory could be a tactic in the pursuit of the goal of security.

A more difficult distinction to make is between *values* or *interests*, and *needs*. This distinction is, as we will discover, important in the explanation of why win–win outcomes are possible. Values and interests relate to those goals of individuals, parties and cultures that are specific, they form a hierarchy and are subject to change in hierarchial order. Needs relate to those goals that are universal — they are those that are sought by all persons, in all cultures and in all circumstances. They are not so subject to repression or devaluation. We make only the distinction now; later each set will be described more precisely.

There appears to be a tendency in conflict settlement to refer to the total relationships of all parties taken together. The United Nations refers to 'the Middle East' situation and 'the Cypriot' dispute, and appoints mediators in relation to those total situations. We refer to the 'British Rail' dispute. As a consequence there is a tendency to group together all the parties into two main opposing factions — Israelis and Arabs, Greek and Turkish Cypriots and the supporters on each side, workers and management. In a problem solving mode there are many parties and there are issues that are specific to different parties. Conflicts must be broken down into their component parts before the total situation can be analyzed and defined. The issues are those that the parties perceive, not those determined by any third party. Hence, it is appropriate to refer to a set of disputes comprising many *parties* and *issues*. This phrase has, therefore, the specific meaning of the issues that relate to separate parties as perceived by the parties.

Other special uses of language will occur. We are generally not only unfamiliar with the concept of problem solving, but we may well argue that problem-solving does not exist in the win-win sense in which we use this term. It could well be argued that 'win-win' is a meaningless concept to those engaged in conflict. Certainly our experience and culture have drawn us in the direction of bargaining processes. Our language is the language of power and power bargaining. It is the purpose of this manual to give meaning to the notion of problem solving by giving explanations of why win-win is a realistic outcome to most conflicts and by detailing the processes involved.

THE SETTLEMENT PROCESS

The settlement process has acquired the description, 'the art of the possible'. Behind this phrase lurk many assumptions. Clearly it is implied that there are objective conflicts of interest to be mediated — the art is to provide the greatest possible satisfaction and 'face' to the parties. Underlying the assumption that there are objective conflicts of interest is an assumption that conflict is due to scarcity. Inherent in this assumption is a further one that conflict is finally over material goods, for it is these that are in short supply.

The processes of settlement follow on these assumptions. They are essentially processes by which a cake of given size is shared according to legal norms and relative power bargaining.

The ideal process has been regarded as one which is based wholly on legal norms and conducted by courts. These have been notably unsuccessful, especially in international and industrial disputes in which important interests are at stake. The refusal of parties to be bound by court decisions has led to a series of less formal processes — what lawyers call 'weaker' processes: arbitration, and, weaker still, mediation and conciliation. Even these weaker forms carry with them some obligation to accept findings and are, for this reason, not entered into by parties to major disputes. This leaves direct power confrontation or bargaining, often with consequences costly to all parties.

The essential reason why these settlement processes are unacceptable, or fail when pursued, is that parties to major disputes are not willing to hand over their decision making to a third party. Responsible trade union executives and leaders of a nation cannot agree to any third party, be it a court or a mediator, making decisions that affect those whom they represent. Conflict-settling processes, to be effective, must include high levels of participation of the parties concerned and must leave final decision making with the parties right up to the point at which the final agreement is negotiated. The traditional settlement processes provide neither opportunities for effective participation nor effective control of outcomes. In courts, parties are represented by legal advisers and decisions are made by judges. In mediation, the parties frequently do not even meet and the mediator has the role of suggesting the compromise.

When in any walk of life we are faced with failure, it is time to look back at our assumptions. In this case the settlement processes, the means of dividing the cake, followed logically from the assumptions: conflict is due to objective differences of interest and to distribution of scarce material resources. Different assumptions lead logically to different processes.

THE RESOLUTION PROCESS

The resolution process is a logical extension of another set of assumptions which experience suggests are more related to political realities.

It is true that parties to disputes, whether industrial, international or other, regard their conflicts as being of a win–lose kind and set out to win. It is also true that in describing their conflicts they refer to material goods in short supply, such as wages, or symbols and roles that cannot be shared (for example, sovereignty). Courts and mediators have no option, it seems, but to take the conflict as defined by the parties and arbitrate or mediate on this basis.

In practice the stated issues in conflict rarely reveal the main goals and concerns. Wage demands are prompted by a sense of injustice — a denial of distributive justice — by feelings of resentment caused by 'we–they' relations and many such rarely articulated motivations. Evidence that this is the case is the relatively low incidence of industrial conflict among small firms where there is a close face-to-face relationship. International conflicts may be stated in terms of territory, as in the Middle East, or 'foreign interference', as was the case in Iran. The real issues relate to security, recognition and identity. The diplomatic threat and bargaining processes do not reveal the hidden concerns. Judicial settlements, if they were to be sought, would take into account legal norms, not these underlying influences on behaviour.

As a consequence experience leads us to consider some radically different assumptions. Conflict may not be over material goods and symbols that cannot be shared, but over commonly held or universal goals such as identity, recognition, a sense of control through effective participation, security and such basic needs that we know are a part of the human developmental process.

These needs are 'social goals' that, unlike material resources, are not in short supply. The more security one party experiences, the more others experience. The more identity a minority ethnic group experiences, the more likely it is to accord recognition to others and to cooperate within an agreed social and political system. Greek Cypriot attempts to impose a constitution that made 'nameless people' out of Turkish Cypriots were doomed to failure. Israeli attempts to make second-class citizens out of Palestinians are also doomed to failure.

If this is the case then, clearly, it is in the interest of all parties to ensure that the opposing parties achieve these social needs. Israelis, Greek Cypriots, Protestant Irish, white South Africans can achieve their basic goals of security by ensuring their opponents have their identity, recognition and security. This is not idealism. It is just practical political realism. It applies to industry also.

It follows that the law and order approach, the application of coercion, cannot produce security and cannot lead to socialization and conformity. If identity, recognition, security and participation are deeply ingrained human needs, they will out — regardless of repression, threat or coercion.

If this is so, then the resolution process must be such that these underlying motivations are brought to the surface and revealed by the parties to each other. The process must enable the parties to differentiate tactics from goals. The process must correct any misperceptions created by the language used which often means one thing to a local population and another to others, and it must give parties opportunities to explore options and not just bargain over stated positions. This implies an analytical approach — the reason why the process has been labelled a 'workshop'.

THE ENTRY PROBLEM

Experience is that once conflict has occurred the parties are reluctant to continue consultations or come together in order to discuss their problems. The first action Britain took in response to Argentine occupation of the Falklands was to break off diplomatic relations. It is general practice to withdraw diplomats at a time of acute disagreement. The smallest diplomatic missions are with 'enemy' countries and the largest with 'friends and allies'. Diplomacy is a confrontation and bargaining process and gives place to more direct forms of conflict.

Similarly, the UN has failed to provide a forum or framework in which the analytical process can take place. Its institutions are a public extension of the private confrontation processes of diplomacy. Nor has the UN Secretariat succeeded in institutionalizing problem-solving processes. On the contrary, its appointed mediators and its own staff have confined themselves to the traditional processes of mediation, that is, going from one side to the other with proposals and compromises until failure has made this irrelevant.

Diplomats are withdrawn, and the traditional mediation processes fail to bring parties together, because parties are not prepared to weaken their bargaining positions by 'recognizing' the opposing party or by entering into discussions on any basis other than the one they establish. The Cypriot parties could not be brought together because each would meet only on the basis of the rival constitution it supported. Britain would not meet with the Argentine until forces were withdrawn from the Falklands. Israel will not meet Palestinians because this would give status and recognition to them. This gives the mediator no option but to practice 'shuttle diplomacy'. In due course he loses the confidence of all parties as he urges compromise and acceptance of *his* proposals.

As a consequence, there is in the world society no legitimized institution to which parties can come when involved in conflict. Courts, arbitration, mediation, direct bargaining are held to be irrelevant and, indeed, dysfunctional and likely to lead to escalation of conflict and hardening of positions.

The question arises, therefore, as to whether conceivably there can be any institutional framework in which parties in conflict — even in violent conflict — can meet together, in the presence of a third party, to analyze their relationship and to explore options. The question can be posed in another way. Is there any institutional framework in which parties can meet without in any way prejudicing their power and bargaining positions, without attracting charges of appeasement, without making it appear that they are too readily seeking peaceful solutions?

Any such institutional framework would have, first, to be outside the realms of power political relations and, therefore, outside the realms of diplomacy and inter-state institutions such as the UN, otherwise problems of status and recognition would crop up.

Second, any such framework would have to enable parties to explore freely without commitment, without implied obligations to arrive at solutions, and probably without giving up any military or other bargaining position they may hold.

Third, any such framework would have to ensure that the parties were and remained their own decision makers, with equality of free decision making, right to the point of agreements.

Fourth, any such framework would have to ensure an

outcome that satisfied not only the parties as defined, but also their own electorates, including their oppositions.

In the field of emergency and disaster there is the Red Cross and similar organizations. Their services are sought by parties to disaster. Their legitimization is not based on any inter-state agreement or any state sponsorship. Their legitimization is based on their professional status and the total control of their activities by the host state which has invited them. A conflict resolution or facilitating service would need to have its legitimacy simiarly based on its professionalism and the service it could provide.

There is no such institution in world society. There is no body to which parties to disputes can come — except informal religious and private bodies that frequently endeavour to 'mediate', usually in a traditional fashion.

This is a serious gap. The question we are posing is whether the gap must exist because of the refusal of parties to meet and to discuss their conflictual relationships — or whether the institutions and processes that have been offered to parties to disputes are irrelevant and inappropriate. Is it possible to create an institution that meets the above four exacting conditions? This is 'the entry problem'. 'The entry problem' is not solved until parties themselves, by their own initiative, *seek* 'a service'. It is probably a myth that parties to conflict prefer to fight it out. The more likely explanation why they continue in conflict is that they perceive no options. Until there is the appropriate institution parties will not seek a facilitating service.

THE INSTITUTIONALIZED WORKSHOP

There have been many occasions in which parties to disputes have met in an analytical framework. Because it is analysis and exploration that is required, these occasions have tended to be semi-academic, that is, meetings that comprise scholars and practitioners.

For example, the Test Ban Treaty was explored at a meeting in Moscow in 1962 by a large number of USA, Soviet and other scholars who had direct links to government. In 1964 there was a meeting in London between nominees of the governments of Malaysia, Singapore and Indonesia, during the violent Borneo dispute. The 'third party' was a panel of scholars. Similarly, there was a meeting in London in 1966 between nominees of the President (Greek) and Vice-President (Turkish) of Cyprus. Since then there have been many meetings between parties to disputes, including Middle East parties, at a lower level of 'representation', at Harvard. More recently there have been facilitated conflict resolution seminars at the University of Maryland relating to the Falklands/Malvinas dispute, and to the problems of Lebanon (see chapter nine).

Such meetings presumably met the four conditions stated above; the parties agreed to meet, they were free to explore and without commitment. They were not without significant results.

As these quasi-academic meetings were possible, it would suggest that the belief that no resolution processes are possible is a false one. Are there non-research, applied practices that meet the requirements?

The nature of a conflict resolution process requires an academic input because it is analytical and exploratory. It requires the injection of whatever knowledge and insights are available. It is for this reason that a panel is required, supported by a wider circle of relevant scholars. It requires, nevertheless, a close connection with relevant authorities.

This presents some practical and cultural problems. Western culture holds government and scholars at a distance from each other. Practitioners are sceptical of and resent the interventions of scholars and scholars fear identification with the ideologies and policies of government. This is less the case in many other societies. Indeed, Western Europe is coming to be the exception. While the same resistances are in evidence in the USA, closer links between government and scholars are developing. In the Soviet Union, China and the developing Third World, the interactions are closer.

This suggests that international networks of scholars could provide a facilitating service, at least until the conceptual notions of problem solving and resolution become more a part of conventional wisdom. However, scholars would not need to perform this role alone. Already in the USA, for example, the processes of resolution are becoming commonplace in industrial and community relations. It is not an accident that the 'Peace Academy' idea was put before the Congress in 1982 and attracted wide support in both houses. The evidence put before the commission of inquiry was strongly along lines of resolution. However, the main experience has been by scholars by reason of their research activities.

The structure of an institutionalized service emerges. It would seem to comprise a substantial group of scholars and practitioners from government, industry and other callings, supported by panels of professionally trained facilitators who could become available as required. The central body, comprising scholars and practitioners from the great powers and others, would seek:

1. To establish an on-going seminar on international relations — in all its aspects. This should be a seminar at which the most recent thinking is examined and a continuing synthesis produced and communicated to practitioners.
2. To make a continuing examination, with a theoretical framework, of the current international situation.
3. To give attention to particular crisis situations as they emerge and to the strategic implications of each.
4. To endeavour to place any existing negotiations, such as SALT, in the wider perspective of great power relations and the wider perspective of developments in the international system as a whole.
5. To establish a panel of trained facilitators.
6. To develop a capacity for problem-solving mediation in any conflict to which attention is drawn by the parties concerned.

THE THIRD PARTY ROLE

This analytical and exploratory approach to disputes can not be undertaken by the parties alone. Experience is that even conflicts within organizations created to resolve problems cannot be resolved by their members! There is always a strong tendency for persons and parties to lapse into a non-analytical bargaining confrontation.

A third party seems to be essential. It is not the third party that suggests compromise or appeals to parties to observe legal norms and moral principles. It is a professional third party that is well informed on all available insights into patterns of behaviour, theories of behaviour, human motivations and goals, the political values attached to status and role and just about everything available in experience and in theory.

This is a demanding qualification. For this reason the third party in a resolution process is not the odd 'experienced diplomat' or acclaimed lawyer. The third party must be a *group* of professionally qualified and experienced persons. Even this is not sufficient. Such a group needs to be in touch with a community of political and social scientists of all kinds to ensure that there is available to the parties all possible relevant information.

There are some personal qualifications required in addition to professional qualifications and knowledge. These are primarily of two kinds.

First, it is preferable that those compromising the third party do *not* have a specialized knowledge of the area and of parties involved in the dispute. The reason for this is that the dispute or conflict is that of the parties. It is for them to define it, and to determine the issues, values and motivations that are relevant. An 'expert' is likely to know the answers before the parties have met!

Second, panel members need to have the capacity to identify with all parties on a no-fault basis — regardless of the apparent 'morality' and values of the parties. They are required to be, and to be seen to be, supportive of all parties.

Experience is that parties first address the panel and try to present their case. It is only when the opposing parties perceive that the third party approves of both them and the opposition that the opposing parties recognize and address each other. This is a direct consequence of the supportive and non-judgemental approach of the third-party panel. Not all persons have these abilities and can refrain from proposing and suggesting at the risk of prejudicing their relationships with the parties.

THE PROCEDURES

The first task of the third party or 'facilitator' is to make a
tentative selection of parties and issues. Typically no conflict is
one between just two parties. Typically there are divisions
within parties and there are, also, external interests. Typically
even the most seemingly simple conflict involves many parties,
each with its own special issues.

It is necessary to make only a tentative judgement as interactions could indicate that those who seem to be the parties most
involved and on whose agreement resolution rests are not the
relevant ones. The guiding principle is that those whose transactions are most threatened or severed are those with whom to
commence — step-by-step broadening out. In the Cyprus case,
the two Cypriot communities are the main parties. Greece and
Turkey are on the boundaries, and the UK, the Soviet Union
and the USA, while indirectly concerned, are less involved. In
the Falklands/ Malvinas case, the Argentine and the UK were
wrongly designated the parties, and negotiations were complicated for this reason. The Falkland Islands and the Argentine
were the parties immediately and directly concerned. Britain
had a legal interest that had to be negotiated once the main
parties had agreed. An agreement between the parties most
involved is likely to be acceptable by other parties — not the
other way around.

A second step is to invite what seem to be the most immediately affected parties to a discussion, while at the same
time taking steps to ensure that other parties appreciate that
their views and interests will not be neglected in subsequent
discussions.

A legitimized body, which like the Red Cross has behind it a
reputation of professionalism and success, would attract invited parties to a dispute. Initially the encouragement of other
powers is necessary. There are compelling reasons both why
great powers would wish to give this support and why smaller
states would wish to respond. Conflicts within the spheres of
interest of the great powers can readily spill over into great
power relations. It is in the relations of all states, great and
small, to deal with problems of change within states and

relations between states, by means that do not risk escalation of conflict between the thermonuclear powers. The tendency in diplomatic negotiation is to endeavour to keep other powers out of conflicts within a sphere of interest. In a conflict resolution process the direct involvement of scholars and advisors from powerful states is functional and part of the wider endeavour to limit conflict and to establish greater cooperation and confidence.

Once assembled, the third party, the facilitator, must set the stage. Parties will have come from a bargaining and often violent conflictual situation. They need to know what is expected of them. One effective means is to explain the resolution process by using the simple diagram employed in the Introduction above. The supportive role of the third party must be made clear.

The agenda is to invite each party to state its position. This takes a characteristic form. An appeal is made by the parties to law, history and morality. The facilitator is the target. The parties, typically, do not address or look at each other.

Then each party is invited to pose questions, strictly for information purposes and not to engage in debate. After this, the panel is in a position to direct questions which seek to uncover aspects of the conflict that have not been touched upon — probably deliberately.

The analytical process continues over some days. Little by little the parties begin to address each other and little by little begin to use the same terminology in redefining the situation. The motives and interests revealed are common — security, identity and others.

During this process it is necessary for the panel members to have frequent and adequate opportunities for discussion among themselves. Different discipline and different backgrounds lead panel members to pick up different points. Different theoretical orientations suggest different procedures. They have to be able to sort out the input from the parties, to synthesize it and to present it back to them. If the panel get it wrong, the parties make this clear and the process continues. If the parties are satisfied with the redefinition, the groundwork has been completed for negotiation.

THE RE-ENTRY PROBLEM

There is great danger that this on-going process that usually lasts a week or so, will alter the values and perceptions of the participants. This would make their 're-entry', their reporting back to those they represent, difficult and perhaps impossible. It is healthy if those opposite each other at the table leave with as much antagonism and prejudice as when they came! Agreement is then on some functional basis that satisfies the interests, needs and goals as perceived by the respective parties.

One precaution the facilitator can take is to make clear when inviting the parties that 'hard-liners', even government opposi-tions, should be included in the teams. Re-entry sometimes depends on such political activists being able to claim a 'win'.

It is part of the role of the facilitator constantly to remind participants of their re-entry problem, of their need not to compromise on key values and to maintain as close contact as possible with those whom they represent.

PRACTITIONER-SCHOLAR COOPERATION

There are occasions in which the workshop principle has to be adapted to the situation, especially when parties to disputes believe that they are guaranteed power support and have no need to undertake any interactions with opposing parties.

Let us take, as an example, the present Middle East situation. While there have been many direct interactions between Israe-lis and Palestinians at an unofficial and informal level, neither side is seemingly prepared to interact with the other for fear of giving ground on declared bargaining positions. Both sides believe they can count on the support of external parties. Yet, in a thermonuclear world, these same external parties cannot afford in their own security interests to be held hostage by their clients. What, then, would be a relevant USA (for example) policy?

The following propositions would seem relevant as the basis of a policy:

1.   The Middle East conflicts can be resolved *only* by the parties concerned and without the external imposition of proposals by any other power.

2.   Those involved comprise many parties and issues, all of which must be taken into account before there is any chance of an acceptable negotiation and resolution. It takes some sorting out which are the parties and issues; the start has to be made with those most directly affected, but all have to be included in a programme of consultation, including possibly the USSR, as wider interests are taken into account.

3.   The issues relate to security, identity, participation and perceived justice and it should be noted that these are not goals that are in conflict; they are shared objectives that all can attain. The more security one experiences, the more others experience. These kinds of goals are not the ones stated by the parties and do not come to the surface in the ordinary processes of diplomatic bargaining.

4.   *Solutions* cannot be *negotiated* until each party fully understands the concerns and claims of the others. This requires a more direct communication than has hitherto been the case.

5.   *Negotiated* agreements imply some degree of compromise or accommodation, as does the working through of many parties at the boundaries of the conflict. However, any finally negotiated agreements must meet the security and ethnic needs of all the peoples: there are some core issues on which there cannot be compromise — power bargaining has to be excluded at all stages for this reason.

6.   The USA should be prepared to assist the parties in these endeavours by providing good offices, communications and opportunities for more direct contact and for informal explorations at all levels including the highest. These explorations by their nature do not and must not be based on prior commitments or any obligations. They are exploratory and do not involve issues of recognition or carry any implications other than those inherent in a mutual willingness to explore relationships.

7.   The USA should explore the processes of this alternative diplomacy with people with experience in them, who could form a panel. Furthermore, they should not look for

one mediator, as they have done, but come to grips with the need for a panel. The panel itself rests on the advice of an even wider network, because the technique requires this kind of group role and wider backing.

8.   The US government would need to sell the approach to the parties by ordinary diplomatic contacts with an assurance that there would be no attempt to force any solution on any party. Prospective panel members would be available to assist in this selling process.

9.   The US government should also intimate that in the context of USA-USSR relations and the world system generally, it is not prepared for ever and a day to go on guaranteeing the status quo in the absence of a serious attempt by the parties to explore their relationships by such processes.

10.   If there were some measure of success and stability, the USA would be prepared to contribute extensive economic support for purposes of transition and establishment of the new structures that would emerge.

Whether or not this would be an acceptable USA policy toward the Middle East, it demonstrates the way in which the authorities and scholars can work together. However, before this can happen or is likely to happen, there has to be a a recognition of the fact that the facilitator role is a professional one and not one that diplomats can enact without training. Just as legal and technical advice is sometimes sought, so must such facilitating advice be sought in a conflict situation.

A PARADIGM SHIFT

We commenced with the 'realist' view that conflict involves objective differences of interest, that it is over scarce resources, usually material resources, that the processes of settlement must be, therefore, means of dividing the cake of given size.

We have advanced a different set of assumptions that lead to quite different processes. It is useful to list the two different sets of assumptions.

TWO PARADIGMS

Set A	Set B

Analytical Assumptions

Set A	Set B
1. Scarcity of resources renders human conflictual relations inevitable.	1. Human relations are dominated by exchange of social goods that increase in supply with consumption — identity, ethnicity, recognition, stimulation, participation, development.
2. Conflict is objective because of scarcity.	2. Conflict is subjective because of hierarchies of values that alter with perceptions and altered relationships.
3. Conflict is win-lose in its outcome.	3. Conflict is perceived as win–lose but because it is subjective has potential positive sum outcomes.
4. Relative power and bargaining power determine proportions in win–lose outcomes.	4. Power cannot be defined and outcomes are indeterminate.
5. Due to scarcity humans have evolved as aggressive.	5. Humans maximize their goals by responding to the environment to the best of their abilities within limits imposed by structural conditions and knowledge of possible options open.

6. Conflicts are settled by relative power and/or by the application of legal norms.

6. Conflicts are *settled* but not *resolved* by coercion.

7. Individual values are subordinate to institutional or social values.

7. When institutional values and human needs are in conflict, the latter prevail.

8. Authorities have a right to expect obedience and others a duty to obey.

8. Authority finally rests on values attached to relationships between authorities and those over whom authority is exercised.

9. Deviance of all types requires separate analysis and treatment.

9. Deviance and 'legal' behaviour are not different forms of behaviour and should be analysed within the same behavioural framework.

10. Authorities owe their legitimacy to effective control and foreign recognition.

10. The legitimacy of authorities is derived from those over whom the authority is exercised.

11. The role of authorities is to preserve the institutions and values of the society.

11. The role of authorities is to manage relationships so that human needs are satisfied.

12. Deterrence and coercion control deviant behaviour.

12. Deterrence as a control of behaviour is confined to threatened loss of or damage to valued relationships and, without the prior existence of such relationships, it has no effective power of control.

13. Processes of judicial settlement, arbitration, mediation, conciliation and good offices are adequate means of settling conflicts.

13. Confrontation processes fail to separate tactics and goals; they seek the application of norms or compromises but not resolutions of conflict.

14. Decision making is necessarily reactive and hierarchical.

14. Effective decision making is interactive, i.e. parties affected are participants in the decision-making process.

15. Structures and institutions are the appropriate units of analysis or explanation of political phenomena.

15. The individual identity group is the appropriate unit of explanation of political behaviour at all system levels.

Process Assumptions

16. Mediation is an art; there are 'born' mediators who cannot pass on their techniques; success is measured by the reputation of the mediator as diplomat or lawyer and not by his performance, for this is determined by the complexity of the situation.

16. Mediation is a learned technique and performance is measured by success and failure.

17. The personality of the mediator is the important consideration.

17. Personal temperament is relevant to all occupations, but the presence or absence of learned techniques is the important consideration.

18. The mediator requires power support from an international institution, powerful states or financial institutions.

18. There is a difference between enforced settlement and resolution of conflict and the latter is accomplished without support except respect for the professional knowledge and status of the mediator; authority is derived from the parties and not from external institutions.

19. It is part of the role of the mediator to suggest solutions.

19. It is only the parties that can arrive at solutions and the mediator should never prejudice his position by suggesting them.

20. The mediator's genius is in suggesting reasonable and workable compromises.

20. No party should ever be asked to accept a compromise and the mediation exercise is to arrive at alternative goals or means that do not require compromises.

21. The interest of greater powers and world society as a whole must sometimes be placed before the interests of the parties.

21. In any conflict, the relations of the parties most directly concerned take precedence and are then subjected to the resolution of any conflict they have with interests at other levels.

22. Relations between states are relations between authorities within them and mediation must be between authorities involved in a conflict situation.

22. World society is not comprised of states as separate entities, but of transactions of all kinds that cut across state boundaries; mediation must be at different levels involving

parties and different issues, sometimes parties within parties and not only legal authorities.

23. International conflict is separate from domestic conflict.

23. International conflict is usually a spill-over from domestic conflict in which parties seek foreign assistance. Mediation must involve domestic consideration of ethnic and other groups and not be confined to international conflict.

24. Parties 'should' accept processes of arbitration and mediation.

24. No party can be expected to submit to third-party judgements or be involved in processes which place it in a position of having to accept a consensus view. Failure to accept some form of arbitration or mediation is a reflection on the mediation process and is not evidence of a party's unwillingness to resolve the conflict or to cooperate in a world society.

25. Some decision makers behave 'irrationally'.

25. Parties to a conflict are responding to the situation in the ways that appear most beneficial to them in light of the knowledge they have of the motivations of others and the options open: 'irrational' behaviour is behaviour not understood or approved by others.

26. No fixed procedures are possible.

26. A disciplined adherence to rules of procedure is desirable once they have been tested.

27. The mediator should be one person.

27. The mediator needs to be a panel of specialists in the field of conflict.

8 Lessons for Great Power Relations

Edward E. Azar and John W. Burton

THE STATE AND THE IDENTITY GROUP

Civilisations face a complexity of apparently unrelated problems — inflation, unemployment, inner-city riots, drunken-
ness and drugs, racial conflict, mugging, terrorism, corruption,
communal conflict, ideological conflict, wars and arms escalation, famine, poverty — to name some of the more serious.

Each is perceived to be a separate problem and remedies are
ad hoc.

It is not likely to be coincidental that problems such as these
are universal, are becoming more severe, and tend to occur at
all these different social levels simultaneously. The probability
is that all have common origins.

A holistic explanation of such social and political problems
tends to be reductionist and so generalized as to be meaningless, for example, the nature of man, immorality, greed or false
value systems. Yet a holistic approach to problems seems to be
required if there is to be understanding and explanation
leading to solutions: specialized approaches and narrow definitions of problems have failed. There is a need to stand back
from particular problems to obtain a wider perspective, to find
patterns of behaviour that relate one's problem area to others.

In no field of enquiry is this more necessary than in US–
Soviet relationships, for here there has been a focus on particular aspects of the whole to a degree that is not rational even
by ordinary standards of social problem solving. Arms control
negotiations are conducted in the narrow context of the felt
need for arms with little analysis being made of the sources of

this felt need. Behaviours are interpreted without reference to their historical and cultural background.

How can there be a holistic approach to Soviet–American relations within the power political framework that prevails?

In previous chapters it was argued that conflictual relationships have as their origin the denial of human needs. Human needs are widely denied even in the most advanced societies. Conflictual situations emerge when the denial is on a scale or of a kind that is intolerable, as when ethnic identity and culture are threatened. They may emerge even when there are relatively minor denials, such as some forms of discrimination on grounds of race or religion, if there is an absence of the valued relationships with authorities that can offset these demands. We have demonstrated this to be the case by reference to multi-ethnic societies in which the first loyalty is to identity groups rather than to the state. It is identity groups that seek to preserve and to promote common human needs, while it is the state that seeks to impose institutions that reflect sectional interests. Only when the state is also the identity group, or when its institutions and policies, however imperfect, are perceived to cater to basic needs in the given environmental and historical circumstances, is value attached to relationships with it. 'Nationalism', in the sense of loyalty to the state, is a reality only when the state is also, in this sense, the identity group.

However, it should not be thought that we are concerned with ethnicity problems. They are a subset of identity problems, only special examples of a more general proposition. Conflicts in which there are no obvious identity issues involved and which are defined, therefore, in quite different terms, on analysis are seen to have the same root causes that relate to identity, recognition, security and such human needs.

SOVIET–US RELATIONSHIPS

Let us apply the general approach to the particular situation of Soviet–USA relationships. The conflictual situation between the two is labelled ideological. The assumption on both sides is that the other is aggressive and expansionist. Each argues that it is in the interests of humanity that its system should prevail and thus appears to the other as bent on destroying the competing system. As each sees the other as being intent on its destruction, each follows strategic policies that lead to escalating defence. Each side, however, perceives the other's defence as offence.

In the framework which we have advanced there is the alternative explanation of the conflict. This alternative explanation suggests the need for quite different state defence policies, and, also, dispute resolution processes quite different from traditional adversary diplomacy.

This alternative explanation has two components. There is the issue of mutual fear, and the related issue of preservation of identity.

The fear each side has of the other is a fear for the internal survival of its own system. The hypothesis is that if there were more total security internally, there would be no fear of any external intentions or influences.

The US has a confident attitude toward its form of democracy and freedom. There is without a doubt widespread support for it. Migrations show that many would like to live within the same type of system. There are migrations from every state that moves towards communism. At the same time there is a growing disquiet in developed capitalist societies at the failure of economic and financial policies to achieve a prosperous, just and stable society. Kuttner has written of *The Economic Illusion; False Choices between Prosperity and Social Justice* (1984). He has shown that the policies the US and the UK have followed to promote investment and jobs have been self-defeating. The rich get richer and the poor get poorer, permanent unemployment becomes an institution and the cuts in expenditure on education and health seem to be self-reinforcing. Kuttner has argued that a greater redistribution of income and greater expenditure on social services is required, not for reasons of justice, but for reasons of investment and growth.

Kuttner points to the need only for policy changes: the system problem could be solved if policies were directed toward income redistribution. Burton is less optimistic (1984). He has termed '*un*development' the condition Kuttner describes. It is a process that leads to underdevelopment. The social wage is cut as funds for education, medical care and welfare generally are reduced. As Kuttner argues, this leads only to progressive *un*development, offset only in the short term by technological advances. Burton asserts that even when the processes lead to stages at which the *un*development is apparent, as in Britain, no policy change is likely, for the economic system is controlled by those who have an interest in ensuring that there is no redistribution of income or increase in the social wage. As a group the élite may know and believe that policies are leading to *un*development, but as individuals they have a high stake in resisting policy change.

Furthermore, examples of income redistribution elsewhere are perceived by élites as a potential system threat. When neighbouring El Salvador experiences the troubles to be expected within a feudal system, the US feels it necessary to support the repressive regime, rather than to have near its borders a government that would pursue more egalitarian policies, even though these policies might be within a system of capitalism. The fear is that this might bring demands for such reforms in the US itself. It has, therefore, no hesitation in attacking Nicaragua on the grounds that there are constraints on freedom, while it treats Chile as a 'friendly' country.

The overriding consideration in both US and Soviet Union foreign policies is not any human interest, value or need, but system preservation. The fear the US has of the Soviet Union and its 'aggressive expansionism' is a reflection of this internal fear of system failure.

So it is, too, with the Soviet Union. In the communist system the same struggle takes place for industrial investment and production. There, however, distribution is controlled. The problem is not an absence of distributive justice. The problem is an absence of political participation, of opportunity for individual development. There are, as a consequence, the same fears for the system if neighbouring countries give examples of an alternative form of communism. There are the same concerns about alternative systems in neighbouring states where there are the perceptions of external interventions. There is the same belief that the preservation of one's own system is vital for the preservation of human needs. There is the same determination to devote whatever resources are necessary for the preservation of the system. There is the same backing of repressive regimes within one's own sphere of influence.

As within countries in the Third World, external security for the great powers finally rests on their internal security. Legitimization is a key factor in the developed world no less than in the underdeveloped. In the Western democracies, while there is support for the political system, governments and leaders that come to power with considerably less than 50 per cent of the votes of those eligible to vote cannot count on the allegiance of their peoples in adverse conditions. In the Soviet Union, a dictatorship through one party cannot count on widespread support without a great deal of coercion and constraints.

THE IDENTITY ISSUE

While the real interest in both cases is in the preservation of system, and relatively speaking much less the promotion of human needs, the two are related in the perceptions of élites and people generally. In the US, the consensus is that it is the American system which can best preserve and promote human needs. Therefore, system preservation is vital. For this reason the state becomes an identity group and attracts support, at least until system failings become clearly oppressive and affect the lives not only of the old and underprivileged, but also of those who are organized to promote their own interests.

Despite frustrations and denial of participation in the Soviet system, there is a consensus that socialism is the only guarantee finally of justice and development in all its aspects.

Thus the state in each case becomes the identity group in respect to the main issues that are in dispute between them. While both believe that, given the opportunity, there would be demands for change, the reality is that there is in both a consensus that will not break down until the system failings become oppressively evident.

In such circumstances it can be anticipated that competitive expenditures on arms will not weaken the resolve of either side. The conflict must be a protracted one while these perceptions by each side of the other remain.

Empirical evidence, argument and even direct interactions in a negotiating situation will not alter this situation. Indeed, negotiation and ordinary adversary diplomatic contacts tend to reinforce preconceived assumptions. Standing back from the situation, it is clear that the assumption that the Soviet Union is aggressive and seeks to impose communism throughout the world is about as realistic and accurate as the assumption that the motivation of the US is world domination. The number of cases in which the US has intervened in the affairs of other countries by overt or covert means is probably as great as, if not greater, than the number of Soviet interventions. The thesis that there is aggression for its own sake, or for reasons of world domination, is superficial and leads to self-fulfilling policies. The more each side endeavours to constrain or compete with the other, the more the other has to respond.

Attempts to arrive at agreements on arms control in these circumstances cannot succeed. First there would have to be a reduced felt-need for arms. This could come about only through an understanding of the situation in greater depth, and an acceptance of the fact that the real source of insecurity is within states: an acceptance for which leadership and élites will not be ready until system failure is apparent. The response then would probably be an aggressive one directed against the enemy held to be responsible for the failure.

THE NEED FOR ANALYTICAL APPROACHES TO CONFLICT RESOLUTION

In a typical ethnicity-conflict situation, the communities in conflict seek the same values — their identity, the security of their identity and of their culture. They are prepared to fight each other, to seek to dominate each other in any power-sharing system, in the belief that their identity is best preserved by such domination. Each community perceives the other as set to destroy its identity. Given the hypothesis that ethnic identity can be secured only by being dominant, there can be no let-up in a power struggle.

When such parties are brought together, as argued in previous chapters, they discover that they are seeking the same goals, that self-preservation and not expansionism is the real motive, and that each party values its relationships and exchanges with the other. The conflict is not a win-lose one. Given the appropriate institutions each can achieve its goals and at the same time take advantage of the benefits of the interactions and ordinary commercial and cultural exchanges.

This could well be the case in Soviet–US relationships. It is possible to explain Soviet behaviour in terms that have little to do with aggressiveness or communism. There are three influences in Soviet policies. First, over a long period of time Russia was the target for invasion. After the revolution, the fear of invasion was not helped by Western attempts to suppress the new regime. It should be recalled that even at the beginning of World War II, Churchill would not refer to the USSR as an ally, not until it had successfully resisted Hitler's invasion. The USSR believed that the West delayed the second front in the hope that the Soviet Union would be crippled. This paranoia has a sound foundation in history and experience.

Second, the Soviet Union is an underdeveloped economy. Much of what goes on within the Soviet Union: shortages, overcrowding in accommodation, poor working conditions, is not a function of communism but of underdevelopment. In fact, of the underdeveloped countries the Soviet Union has been the most successful, largely because of its egalitarian policies. Housing, consumer goods and welfare services have become available to all. However, identity problems and frustration inherent in a lack of a sense of participation are not acceptable in exchange for material welfare. In a study of Libya (Mustafa *et al.*, 1981) it was found that greatly improved physical conditions of life do not automatically lead to an improvement in the psychological quality of life.

Third, the Soviet Union, Russian in character, has a cultural base of authoritarianism. Communism is not more authoritarian than previous regimes. Respect for authorities is deeply ingrained, no matter what opinion is held of them.

In short, what is seen as characteristics of communism by the West is not communist, but Russian: fear of invasion, underdevelopment and authoritarianism. These are conditions with which Soviet citizens and the world society has to live, until greater political stability in Europe and Asia give a greater sense of security, until there is development and until these altered conditions make possible a greater participation in internal affairs.

Similarly, it can be argued to Soviet observers that what appears to be US aggression and expansionism is explicable in terms of the history of the West and of the US in particular, its progressive movements from most oppressive institutions of slavery, feudalism, colonialism and élitism toward social, political and economic institutions that allow for increasing individual development.

The alternative perspective we are here putting forward suggests that East–West and ideological conflicts are essentially the same as ethnicity conflicts. Both are special cases of identity conflicts. In all cases the problem is how to demonstrate the hidden data of common motivation and intent to the parties concerned beyond any doubt, and without giving away the 'security' they have sought through power.

In both cases, what has to be avoided is a freeze on processes of change toward more liberal systems, caused by mutual fear. The trends toward *un*development in the developed Western states would be easier to counter if there were not a Western paranoia. Trends toward greater participation in the Soviet Union would be easier to promote if there were not a similar Soviet paranoia.

In so far as this is the case, Soviet–US relationships are less a matter for strategy and deterrence and more a problem to be solved by analytical means. The underlying motivations and intentions may well be almost identical — as is the case in an ethnicity conflict. Whether this is so or not can never be revealed in a bargaining and negotiating framework. An analytical approach to conflict resolution may reveal realities not brought to light within a bargaining framework.

THE CONFLICT RESOLUTION PROCESS

Academic discussion is not a means to ascertain the hidden data. Scholars are products of their environments and share the assumptions of political élites. Some of the 'scholarly' literature in this area is little more than ideological argument couched in academic terms and in academic style, relying on carefully selected empirical data that supports the ideological contention.

What is required is a process that enables the examination of concepts in depth, the kind of exercise labelled 'abduction' by the Harvard student Peirce at the end of the last century (Levi, 1980). Everything must be up for questioning. What are 'democracy', 'legitimacy', 'freedom', 'justice', 'development'?

Other chapters in this book deal with the problem-solving approach to conflict resolution and its application. Experience has been, to date, largely with conflicts in which ethnicity, language and religion have been the apparent issues. Underlying them are the more fundamental issues of human needs which are discovered by the parties only in a controlled interactive situation. We argue in this chapter that East–West conflict is no different in kind. The same analytical processes are required. The problems before us are how to institutionalize such processes without destroying their nature, how to relate such informal processes to official negotiations, and, above all, how to promote the notion of problem solving instead of confrontation at the inter-state level.

BIBLIOGRAPHY

Azar, Edward E. (1983) 'The theory of protracted social conflict and the challenge of transforming conflict situations', in Zinnes, Dina A. *Conflict Processes and the Breakdown of International Systems.* Denver: Denver University Press.

Burton, John W. (1984) *Global Conflict: The Domestic Sources of International Crisis.* Brighton: Wheatsheaf; College Park, Maryland: Center for International Development, Maryland University.

Kuttner, Robert (1984), *The Economic Illusion: False Choices Between Prosperity and Social Justice.* Boston: Houghton Mufflin.

Levi I. (1980). 'Inductions in Peirce' in Mellor, D. (ed.) *Science Belief and Behavior.* Cambridge: Cambridge University Press.

Mustafe, D.A., Burkart, Holzner and Zoenek, Suda (eds.) (1981), *Directions of Change, Modernization Theory, Research and Realities.* Boulder, Colorado: Westview Press.

9 The Lebanon Case

Edward E. Azar

INTRODUCTION

Two seminars/workshops on conflict resolution in Lebanon were held in May and October 1984 under the auspices of the Center for International Development of the University of Maryland at College Park. These seminars were attended by scholars, political advisers and consultants who were invited to represent the views of the leadership of the Lebanese religious and political communities. Each meeting lasted for four days and featured intensive discussions of the values, needs, issues and expectations of the various communities and the whole nation.

The seminars were analytical encounters between individuals who had been deeply involved, in their different ways, in the internal and regional struggles of Lebanon. During the first meeting, we focused on *whether a united Lebanon* was desired as the homeland for the conflicting Lebanese communities. The second meeting focused on *what kind of Lebanon* was desired. In each case, the participants tried to articulate the positions of the communities to which they belonged and those of the leadership that had nominated them to come to the seminars. At times during these discussions, the participants did not personally hold the views they presented at the conference, but in most instances, there existed a symmetry between the personal views of the participants and the leadership of their communities.

These meetings were intensive efforts to determine the otherwise hidden data of motives, values and intentions. They were carried out without fanfare. The four days of each seminar were fully utilized — from nine in the morning until five or six in the evening participants and panelists were engaged in serious, difficult and frank discussions about all sorts of issues, as shown below.

In the two seminars, the Lebanese participants numbered seven and eight. The Center for International Development panel of experts who facilitated each session numbered four and five. The panel was made up of scholars and practitioners who were specialists in conflict analysis at different levels of social organization, and most were experienced persons in the facilitation of conflict resolution.

These meeting were based on some guidelines regarding theory and process. John Burton (1984) had spelled these out as follows:

1. Ensure that the discussions are 'informal' and do not commit authorities in any way, and for this reason usually are between persons nominated by leaders, but not representing them.
2. Ensure that the discussions are analytical, that is, that they seek to reveal the hidden motives and intentions of the parties and whether assumed motivations and intentions are real.
3. Provide an opportunity to explore possible outcomes in the light of the goals and values revealed, again without any commitments.
4. Take advantage of knowledge available by having a panel as a third party, drawn from several disciplines, and helpful in discovering options that are particularly suited to the situation.
5. Ensure that no party is required to compromise or in any way submit to influence or power in any way that would prejudice its basic needs. To this end bargaining and negotiation are avoided.

Burton had written that this process is welcomed by parties to disputes and, furthermore, leads to exciting and unanticipated discoveries about the motivations and intentions of the parties. It has revealed that conflicts that the parties believe to be unique have many features in common with others: there are basic needs of security, identity and control that emerge in all conflicts. This proved to be the case in the Lebanon seminars.

What, then, was revealed at these two intensive seminars on conflict resolution in Lebanon?

THE DYNAMICS

In the first meeting it emerged that the participants had not been able to communicate with each other across the Green Line in Beirut. While most of them were professors who write a great deal about their community and nation, they had not had direct, face-to-face meetings to discuss their ideas, differences and points of view. They had not exchanged their writings, articles and books with one another. During the first meeting, as we, the panel, passed out handouts regarding the seminar, we observed individual participants on both sides of the table exchanging notes and papers with one another. Words of thanks for this gesture were also exchanged as persons on both sides had finally obtained each others' writings to examine and read.

In the second meeting, where there was 20 per cent participant overlap, and where there had been some communication prior to coming to the US, the two sides were less surprised by the presence, ideas, writings, etc. of one another. During this meeting, however, they exchanged books, pamphlets and articles, revealing that they had not been communicating their ideas and points of view in any systematic manner.

At both meetings, the first day, and especially the first session, was spent by each participant setting out the conditions under which he came to these meetings. Moslem participants spent more time spelling out their reasons and parameters for participating in these seminars. Christian and Moslem participants wanted to make it clear that, while they came from certain communities and had been nominated by leaders of these communities, they had their own views and wanted that clearly understood at all times. Needless to say, the participants were very sensitive on the point of their personal views versus that of the leaders who dispatched them to these seminars. Where they agreed with their communal leaders and the general public in their community they wanted that affirmed also. The second and third days of each seminar were more difficult. High levels of tension filled the air, emotions were revealed in no uncertain terms, and deadlocks were encountered at different times. In these latter instances facilitation and constructive intervention were deemed appropriate and necessary.

Participants were neither asked nor expected to engage in a simulation of sorts. None was asked to give up his view or alter it so as to satisfy the other side or members of the panel. Participants were simply encouraged to see the values of the other side as authentic and real.

The last day of each of the seminars was characterized by nervousness and worry. The participants appeared to want to go back home with concrete ideas and accomplishments. They wanted their differences asserted and their performance commended. Many of them, especially during the last session of the seminar, tended to express some cynicism about the *real* intentions of one another. Almost all of them expressed concern about how to agree and on what points, how to disagree and on what points and what to take back home and defend effectively.

The re-entry problem is not an easy one. There are many concerns about it and we share them. However, the level of confidence and trust which were nourished by the panel and participants must have been important.

Almost all the participants, however, expressed the desire to maintain linkages and to create an informal network back home. Many of them made positive statements regarding one another, in private and public settings. Most became hopeful that there exist others on each side who would be good partners in a full national reconciliation effort. Every one of the participants appeared to be eager to become a party to any reconciliation effort in Lebanon. Several of them had expressed many regrets about not having had meetings of this kind before the war started or during the early days of it.

THE ROLE OF THE PANEL

The panel's role was well defined and significant. It remained neutral and facilitative throughout. The main task of the panelists was that of questioning and making observations that had a general application. In conflict resolution seminars of this type, it is the parties that are the experts on their situation and it is they who determine relevance. Thus facilitation in these circumstances is no more than a device whereby parties involved can discover for themselves the hidden data of motivations and intentions. They need the assistance, however, of a panel that knows the kind of questions to ask to ensure that the parties do in fact reveal the true nature of their relationships.

Early encounters in these Track Two Diplomacy conflict resolution seminars must not become bargaining and negotiating situations. In the Lebanese case thus far, the panel thought it necessary to focus the discussion on the 'needs conflicts' and to sort out the hidden data and not allow the group to get diverted into bargaining. Eventually, however, the participants will have to dwell on 'interest conflicts' where a good deal of bargaining and negotiations will be needed.

When problems arose, the panel introduced empirical data about cases other than the Lebanese in which the similarities or differences were instructive for the participants. These interventions in terms of experience and findings were very important. At times, a deadlock was ended by the portrayal of the experience of other societies with identity-driven protracted conflicts such as Cyprus, Northern Ireland, Spain, India, Sri Lanka, etc. When solutions were proposed and found problematic, the panel introduced valid data from other cases where similar solutions were proposed or adopted. In these situations fresh ideas began to emerge and in some cases creative approaches to the problem began to appear on each side. The panel's low-profile role and the use of comparative data and theory were most significant in this process.

Both of these seminars were held in private, under an academic umbrella. No publicity or showmanship was permitted, for confidentiality was deemed essential. When participants themselves became convinced that public knowledge was not only acceptable but necessary, the panel concurred. At the end of the second seminar it was agreed that there should be a publication of the substantive and theoretical ideas presented in these sessions.

THE FIRST MEETING

Our first seminar in May 1984 focused on the fears and goals of the different communities and the means by which there could be cooperation in the reconstruction of a new Lebanon without the sacrifice of the values and the security of any community.

Valuable conclusions were reached. The most significant agreement was that, without qualification, all valued and identified with the State of Lebanon: its independence and development was given the highest priority, subject only to the preservation of the security and values of all.

The following were the shared needs and values and the conflicting interests.

I.   *Shared Needs and Values* (not specifically agreed but inherent in the statements made)
Security
Personal and physical security
Preservation of communities as identity entities
Security of each community from external and internal fear
Durability of any agreed outcome
Identity
Personal identity with confessional community
Identity with Lebanon's special role of a crossroad between
    East and West
Identity with Arabs as a people
Equality
Equality of political participation
Economic equality of opportunity: distributive justice
Developmental equality as between regions
Participation and Control
Values and needs of people should determine structures

Leadership should lead in response to demands on them
No community should be marginalized and none should
    have total control: well-being is not possible unless
    accessible to all
Freedoms
Speech
Belief
Movement

II. *Conflicting Interests*
Political power and built-in security provisions
Economic privilege
Leadership roles
Property rights
Displaced (internal refugee) rights
Wartime interests and roles

Having established these common values, it was easily
agreed that Lebanon should be independent, and removed
from regional conflicts, while maintaining and developing its
commercial, cultural and other links with the outside world.

While it was agreed that religious affiliations are an
important feature of Lebanese society and that such affiliations determine political behaviour in that country, it was also
recognized that there is a national culture with its special
features. Lebanon, by reason of its multi-religious structure
and the historic interactions between different communities,
has developed a culture and a set of values that enable it to
identify with both Christian and Islamic civilizations, while
not being identical with either.

For this reason Lebanon can be a member of the Arab
League and influence its policies, and at the same time be in a
position to interpret Arab politics and concerns to the West.

Frequently, the discussions revealed a concern about relations with Syria, Israel and the US. It appeared that Christians
were unhappy about their past relations with Israel and
Muslims were disappointed with the Lebanese government's
apparent need to rely so much on Syria. The actions of both
sides were described as incompatible with the agreed and

shared value attached to an independent Lebanon, having its own unique culture.

The discovery of a common value attached to Lebanese nationalism, and a common willingness to preserve the values of the different communities, led to the observation that past political compromises and institutions were not appropriate for the satisfaction of emerging communal needs and grievances. Different opinions were expressed as to what structural changes should be introduced in Lebanon. It was, however, agreed that whatever decentralization or public administration changes were introduced, these should address the grievances of the various communities and reflect the goals and values of the whole Lebanese society. It was thought possible and useful that the local administration in Lebanon be expanded and given greater say in the local affairs of people.

It was agreed that this process of discussion facilitated by a panel of scholars was an appropriate one in the circumstances, for it enabled the participants to interact under controls that ensured that the discussions were exploratory, that they focused on the fundamental needs and values of the people of Lebanon, that experience drawn from other situations was available and that important issues would not be hidden or avoided.

It was agreed that further meetings of this kind should take place with the least possible delay.

THE SECOND SEMINAR

Our second seminar in October, 1984, focused on what kind of Lebanon do the Lebanese want for themselves. This question was not fully addressed although some major steps were taken in this direction. The seminar was concluded with a declaration by the participants outlining some interim steps and some long-term concerns.

    1.   In the hierarchy of political values, the highest is in the preservation and development of the State of Lebanon.

    2.   By a Lebanon State is meant a united, Arab, inde-

pendent state which is a meeting ground of Christianity and Islam.

3. The State of Lebanon should develop into a non-communal political system.

4. No community can accept political structures as solutions when they are based on force.

5. In the preservation and development of the State of Lebanon as defined, unless the basic needs of security, freedom of movement, identity and distributive justice in all aspects of life are satisfied, there will be continued strife.

6. In the transition from war to stability, it is necessary not merely to control violence, but to take positive steps to re-establish citizen relationships within and among identity groups.

7. It is only the unity of the Lebanese and Lebanon, embodied in a national consensus, that finally is a defence against external pressures and interventions.

8. It is acknowledged that the need for security may lead to tactics that tend to destroy the independence of Lebanon. The above definition of the united and independent Lebanon implies an obligation on all who support it to refrain from seeking external alliances in their quest for security through power.

9. It is the role of the government of Lebanon and its armed forces to provide physical security to persons and to communities within Lebanon.

10. The armed forces of the government of Lebanon should be under the command of government authorities, and should be reformed, retrained, and re-equipped for their policing role, and could cooperate with local forces and police until such a time as local forces become redundant.

11. The integrity, unity and preservation of Lebanon finally rest on social justice and equality of citizens before the law, regardless of religion, race, colour, sex or social status.

12. Justice requires (a) that all kidnapped persons should unconditionally be freed; and (b) that all Lebanese displaced citizens should have the opportunity to return to their previous abodes as soon as security permits.

13.   Pending an effective transition from war to peace, a third party, agreeable to all, may be required to mediate power rivalries and to reduce the incidence of violence.

14.   Extremist elements, that is, elements that do not share the above definition of a united Lebanon and which work for foreign movements and governments, must be contained.

15.   Transition steps are not complete in the absence of a clear vision of future political, social and economic reforms which are to be ratified by a freely elected representative body.

16.   Immediate decisions are required as to the duties and powers of the national legislative, executive, judicial and local authorities, around which appropriate structures should be constructed.

17.   The transition from war to stability and peace requires the recognition of the authority of the existing political coalition of leaders and their mutual cooperation.

18.   Alterations in the distribution of authority within the political system are required to give a real and a perceived equality of influence to the two main groups.

19.   Decisions by the legitimate government should be implemented faithfully and immediately.

20.   Stability and peace in Lebanon will contribute to a just and lasting peace in the Middle East.

21.   Social stability and peace require a major programme for social, economic, psychological and moral rehabilitation of groups and individuals that have been affected by war and their re-integration into Lebanese society.

22.   Lebanon's economic base is facing decline. The political and social goals stated herein have no possibility of success without a speedy solution to the impending economic crisis in the country.

The following measures are critical: (a) the restoration of the authority of the state in the economy; and (b) the urgent and vigorous implementation of plans for reconstruction, investment and development.

COMPARING SOME ASPECTS OF THE TWO SEMINARS

One of the most important features of both meetings was the preoccupation of both sides with history and their own subjective interpretations, the differences which each side placed on the meaning of events, processes, decisions, and the roles of persons and groups in inter-communal, national Lebanese and regional history. (This is typical in face-to-face encounters, and facilitators must re-direct attention to the underlying causes of conflict.) Another related preoccupation was that of local v. regional nationalisms. These are not new to any Lebanese and have been especially strong in the past decade, and they should not be surprising to students of protracted social conflict either. The history of nationalism reflects the intra-societal and cultural struggles we refer to as identity-driven conflicts.

All participants at both meetings asserted time and again their loyalty to Lebanon as a final homeland and affirmed Lebanese nationalism as desirable without being prejudicial to other allegiances.

This preoccupation was a reflection of underlying distrust. Whereas the issue of national allegiance looked simple on the surface, it was clear that many other hidden problems exist. Every time the participants could not agree, whether on a trivial or significant issue, they would resort to doubting each other's nationalism. The Moslems would argue that reference to Lebanese nationalism camouflaged Christian hegemony, and the Christians would argue that Moslem acceptance of Lebanese nationalism hid the Moslems' true intentions and their strategy of buying time in order to take over the state and its institutions, and to reduce Christians to second-class status. Discussions on history and nationalism easily turned into a discussion about the fears and distrust of each side.

The lack of concern with the past or future roles of Syria, Israel and the US was an interesting feature of the second seminar. In the first seminar in May 1984, Syria, Israel and the US were brought into the discussion at all times. Very often, these three states were blamed for almost everything that went wrong in Lebanon. During the second seminar, domestic determinants of the conflict were discussed at length and the regional and international variables were virtually ignored, thus reflecting the transformation in the balance of forces in Lebanon and the region.

This emphasis in October 1984 was an unexpected event. After so many years of Lebanese dependence on external forces we expected it would be difficult for most Lebanese to face their own actions and dependence behaviour. They did talk about the need for external support to assist the Lebanese authorities to establish the modalities for communal security, personal safety and the rule of law. Some participants were more specific in naming the UN and Syria as capable of providing security support for the immediate future.

The reference to external parties to the Lebanese conflict was full of contradictions, remorse and anger. Each side tended to accuse the external supporters of the other as full of malice. The participants were critical of themselves for having sought external support in their internal struggles. They appeared to be cognizant of the helplessness which had beset them as a result of the decade of war and the decades of dependence on external forces and alliances to tip the domestic scales. While they all wanted external parties to lend a helping hand to stabilize the country, most of them saw external parties as the source of strife and violence more than the agents of reconciliation and coexistence.

Participants appeared to have come to grips with the notion that winning in the Lebanese context is a more complicated process than in conventional situations. They seemed to be preoccupied at times with self-discovery. They often talked about their responsibilities towards promoting peace and prosperity in Lebanon without waiting for external parties to participate or take charge. Their discussions revealed a deepening understanding of the dilemmas of hegemony, control, utilization of power, zero-sum games and the like.

It is important to note that the participants tried hard to push their point of view and with great deftness, frankness and politeness. At times they avoided sensitive issues which some members of the panel thought they should tackle. They appeared to prefer to succeed in accomplishing as much as possible and to avoid failure. The concern about succeeding and doing well as representatives of their communities and leaders, and not presenting difficulties, was interesting. That is not to say that all sensitive issues were avoided. On the contrary, some of the most agonizing and difficult issues concerning loyalty to the community, trustworthiness and authenticity of identity were brought up with great frankness. Issues avoided were the present links to external parties and the role of each community in the movement to peace.

AUTHOR'S COMMENTS

The definition of Lebanon's identity and the discussion on what type of society the country develops were highlights in these meetings. They struggled with these for some time. When a solution was arrived at, the two sides appeared to have been surprised at the reaction of one another. The Moslems could not see why the Christians were so concerned about the issues that were raised during the discussion and felt that the Christian position was exaggerated, since they had always been in a leading role in Lebanon. On the other hand, the Christians felt that the Moslems were still being obstinate and unwilling to accept the finality of Lebanon despite all their public pronouncements. The Moslems had been so used to playing second fiddle that they could not believe the Christians were feeling insecure about the economic, demographic and political shifts and their ideological representations in Lebanon and the region. On the positive side the Moslems were pleasantly surprised that the Christians had accepted the definition of Lebanon as an independent, unified Arab country and a meeting place of Christianity and Islam.

The topic that brought them all together was that of the rise of fundamentalism. On this, their fears and that of the state were well articulated. Both sides argued that the problem of extremism needs to be attacked, but how to deal with it became an issue. Immediately the relation of checking fundamentalism was linked to the state and its power and nature. Both sides spoke about the threat of fundamentalism to each community.

Both sides seemed to argue that fundamentalism — and the terrorism that is sometimes associated with fundamentalism — are a function of denial of needs and rights and of fears of anticipated and dark futures. Both sides argued that the lack of national integration and the weakness of the army permit terrorism. The Christians were more adamant about the ability of the Moslem leaders and other external states to check terrorism in the short run. They agreed, however, that in the long run the solution has to stem from within an integrated and united Lebanon with its strong army and police force. The Moslems argued that fundamentalism threatens them just as much as the Christians. They argued that they are the direct victims of terrorism. They stated they could not deal with terrorism because of external links, and because of the skewed and deformed system within Lebanon. Reforms now, and removal of fundamental injustices would, in the long term, deal a blow to terrorism and finally to fundamentalism.

While both agreed that the fears of both sides were genuine, there were doubts about who benefits from these trends in the short and medium run and, therefore, about who is really behind terrorism. Both sides thought that the issue in the long run will be serious to all. The fact that the participants represented the ruling élites in Lebanon may be part of the reason for these attitudes.

The question of fundamentalism, however, was discussed in a way which revealed a contradiction in Lebanon's ability to deal with its political reform issues. Fundamentalism can most probably best be tamed by and through a combination of structural change and increased communal security. However, the participants' preoccupation was with national solutions to Lebanese issues. This will not cope with fundamentalism. The nationalism that the Lebanese participants sought to solve their historical quarrels will most probably promote terror and counter-terror. This situation is paradoxical. If fear of extremism drives Lebanese together, then the conflict of the army v. extremists is likely to get worse: the last thing a Lebanese extremist wants is an *integrated Lebanon*. Thus some of the instruments used to combat terrorism may backfire. Only moderates are seeking nationalism, integration and political reform as a means of checking extremism.

The author feels that the following five issues will continue to derail the Lebanese bandwagon for peace.

1. National identity and constitutional issues;
2. Security, communal militias and the army — how to harmonize these;
3. Structure, central state, local powers and demarcations;
4. Healing the scars of war and promoting positive participation of the young population; and
5. Economic reconstruction and development.

Conflict resolution in Lebanon can be enhanced as follows:

1. Mapping the future should take place so that there are clear goals.
2. Comparative knowledge of cases would help a great deal to overcome obstacles and potential deadlocks.
3. The focus on domestic issues is essential in the immediate future, but it cannot be separated from the regional sources of conflict.
4. The exit from war to peace can be enhanced by conceptualizing two periods: a *transitional* one and a *long-term* one. The long-term period focuses on general principles about structures and institutions. All communities must be engaged in this long term process. The transition period is a short-term one which must focus on designing and defining inter-communal confidence-building measures.

Fundamental reforms take a long time to be formulated and implemented. They require a semblance of law and order before they can become a reality. In the meantime, Lebanon needs a period of transition towards stability and reform. This transition period can be most effective if it develops inter-communal confidence through meetings of all concerned, networking, planning, arguing and agreeing upon solutions to the problems of physical safety and the stability of the economy.

10 Observations of a Diplomat

Ambassador John W. McDonald

This is an exciting book and certainly justifies Dr Edward Azar's and Dr John Burton's enthusiastic introduction when they write about the new developments in the field of conflict resolution that have been taking place over the last few years. I would like to offer some observations on my own experience in negotiation, and then to make a few comments about several of the earlier chapters of this book.

My introduction to international negotiation at the intergovernmental level took place in January 1947, in Berlin, Germany, when I was assigned as a young lawyer to the US Secretariat of the four-power Allied Control Council (US, UK, France and the USSR) which was ruling what is now East and West Germany. There were no books brought to my attention at that time on the art of negotiation or the cross-cultural implications of negotiating the minutes of a just completed meeting of the four-power Law Committee with my Soviet, French and British colleagues. One learned the hard way, by watching, listening and making mistakes. This can be a painful process and it has not changed that much until quite recently.

Now one is almost inundated with books on negotiation and arbitration, but most relate to US domestic situations rather than to international negotiations and almost all seem to have been written by members of the academic community rather than by practitioners. I have noticed that the practitioners don't read about negotiation and the academicians don't practice negotiation. Unfortunately the two professions often seem to be like two ships passing in the night. We at the

State Department are now trying to do something about this situation.

THE CENTER FOR THE STUDY OF FOREIGN AFFAIRS

The Department of State, through its recently created Center for the Study of Foreign Affairs, has become involved in various aspects of conflict resolution. The Center, which is a part of the Foreign Service Institute, the Department's training arm, came into being in November 1982 and part of its mandate is to focus on 'studies in conflict resolution, the prerequisites and techniques of successful mediation and the skills of negotiation'.

One of the Center's first functions was to plan and then host, in June 1983, a two-day symposium on International Negotiation. The conference was designed to begin to bridge the gap between the practitioners and the academicians. Such eminent professors as Roger Fisher, Bill Ury, and Howard Raiffa of Harvard, Bill Zartman of SAIS, Larry Susskind of MIT and Louis Sohn of Georgia and outstanding practitioners such as Fred Ikle, Paul Warnke, David Newsom, Hal Saunders and Jonathan Dean, participated. It was a stimulating first step.[1]

In early 1984, as a follow-up to the conference on negotiation, the Center published a handbook for government officials and private citizens who had been asked to serve as a representative of the US government on one of the thousand official delegations sent out by the State Department each year to participate in international, inter-governmental conferences of a multilateral nature.[2]

The Center also organized and hosted a series of four one-day symposia in 1984 entitled 'Case Studies in Conflict Management'. The first symposium was on the 'Panama Canal Treaty Negotiations', the second on 'The Falklands/Malvinas Islands Dispute', the third on 'Cyprus' and the last on 'Negotiating Zimbabwe's Independence'. In each instance we brought together as many of the actual negotiators as possible and asked the Washington foreign affairs community to participate.

We invited also, as part of the audience, some ten persons resident in the area who had lectured and written on negotiation and who could represent the academic community. The week following each symposium this group met for half a day to critique the process they had watched unfold to see if it was possible to draw some lessons from that negotiation which could be passed on to future negotiators. These four case studies, and lessons to be learned, will be published in mid-1985. This was another effort to close the gap between practitioners and academia.

Over the past three years Tom Colosi, Vice-President for National Affairs of the American Arbitration Association and a true practitioner, has put on a one-week course at the Foreign Service Institute, four times a year, on the Art of Negotiation. This course is designed primarily for the mid-level foreign service officer and gives that officer, through simulations and lectures, the kind of practical experience needed.

In addition, over the past year I have taught two two-week courses on Multilateral Diplomacy and International Organizations to mid-career diplomats. Seventeen per cent of the Foreign Service is engaged full time in multilateral diplomacy and this is the only course offered, to date, to try to make officers better multilateral diplomats.

In early 1985 the Center began to explore yet another facet of the art of negotiation — Track II Diplomacy. The author of that phrase, Joe Montville, is now a member of the Center's staff and his definition is as follows: 'Track Two diplomacy is unofficial non-structured interaction. It is always open-minded, often altruistic and strategically optimistic, based on best case analysis'.[3]

The easiest way for me to remember the difference between Track I and Track II is that I am Track I — representing my government. I, of course, operate formally at the conference table and informally away from the table, but I can never escape the fact that I speak for the government of the United States — and of course no one else ever forgets that either. Track II representatives are private citizens, don't represent their governments and, because they are not instructed delegates, are on their own, working with other private citizens from other countries and have enormous flexibility. That flexibility, if it is unstructured and undirected, can be the undoing of a Track II initiative. It is that very aspect, the 'unguided missile' approach, that worries many diplomats in the Track I arena, leading them to reject the very concept. My response here is that Track II should not be viewed as action taken instead of, but rather in support of, and parallel to, the goals of Track I. I believe that each can and should help the other.

In an effort to expand the mental horizons of many in the Washington foreign affairs community in this field, the Center hosted and organized a one-day symposium, in February 1985, entitled 'Informal Contributions Toward Conflict Resolution, e.g., Track II Diplomacy'.

Joe Montville was the first speaker. He defined Track II, discussed its application to critical issues in today's world, such as Northern Ireland, Cyprus and Sri Lanka, and pointed out the difference between Track I and Track II. Professor Philip D. Stewart of Ohio State University and rapporteur for the Dartmouth Conference since 1972 explained the history of this conference, its US citizen to Soviet citizen approach, and described the positive, on-going impact these informal communications channels have had on US-Soviet relations over the years. John Scali, former Ambassador to the United Nations and ABC News correspondent, described his role during the 1962 Cuban Missile Crisis when, as a private citizen, he acted as intermediary between the KGB and the White House. Professor Roland L. Warren, formerly of Brandeis University and a long-time National Board member of the American Friends Service Committee, described his Track II experiences in Berlin immediately after the building of the Berlin wall and compared the situation of East and West Germany with his recent experience in North Korea. Dr Bryant Wedge, Director for the Center for Conflict Resolution at George Mason University, then discussed his Track II role in 1965 in dealing with the Dominican Republic crisis. The next speaker was Dr Landrum Bolling, currently Rector of the Ecumenical Institute in Jerusalem, who has spent much of his career in the area of private diplomacy. He focused his remarks on the Arab-Israeli dispute and his own role in interacting with

Mr Arafat of the PLO. The last speaker was John Burton, Director of the Conflict Resolution Project at the University of Maryland's Center for International Development. He has spent much of his career in informal diplomacy and dealt on this occasion with his Track II efforts in Lebanon.

I have gone into detail with regard to this symposium in order to give some idea as to the breadth and diversity of the Track II approach and some indication of the areas of conflict that can be addressed.

The Center's primary goal, however, was to convince the practitioners that Track II, skilfully used in parallel with Track I, could often speed up the process of negotiation or even break a stalemate, thereby enabling Track I to move into the formal negotiation process and complete a Treaty, sign a peacekeeping agreement or do whatever was needed, at the government-to-government level. In other words, Track II initiatives should be viewed as one of several important tools available to a Track I negotiator.

We recognize that the Track II symposium was a first step and plan to continue to explore this process.

A CASE STUDIES FRAMEWORK

One can learn a great deal from those members of the academic community who have written and lectured on negotiation. It is equally true that one can learn from studying past negotiations, if those case studies are carefully crafted and go into sufficient detail to allow an examination of tactics as well as strategy.

There follows a series of questions that should be answered by any writer or student of case studies dealing with international, inter-governmental, Track I negotiations. These questions are divided into four stages:

   I   The Pre-negotiation Phase
  II Preparations for Formal Negotiations
 III The Negotiations Themselves
 IV The Post-negotiation Period

146   International Conflict Resolution

If all or most of these questions can be addressed in a case study then I am convinced the negotiator can learn a great deal from the study that can be applied to future negotiations.

I. The Pre-Negotiation Phase

A.   In placing the case study in an historical context, describe at what point each of the parties decided to seek a negotiated solution to the problem rather than to maintain the status quo.

B.   How long was the pre-negotiation phase? Describe the obstacles to the decision to negotiate and what eventually precipitated the decision to act.

C.   What internal and external influences were involved? Third parties? Did parties not directly involved try to slow down or speed up the pre-negotiation process?

D.   To what extent did the parties agree on a definition of the problem and the shape of a possible solution? Did each party know what it would do if there was no agreement?

E.   How did the US define its own role? How was the US position perceived by others?

F.   Were there false starts or did each party have the political will to move into the negotiating phase the first time this was discussed?

II. Preparations for Formal Negotiations

A.   Once a decision had been made to negotiate what further decisions had to be made by the various parties before the negotiations could actually begin?

B.   How was agreement reached on the terms of reference for the actual negotiations? Was the exact purpose of the negotiation spelled out?

C.   How was it decided where and when the negotiations would take place and what form they would take?

D.   Was this a mediation or a negotiation? If a mediation, did the mediator have to stimulate the negotiation process to get it started? Were third-party 'good offices' used?

E. What kind of staff support was necessary? Were there problems over who should attend: as delegates: as observers?

F. Were international organizations, non-governmental organizations or the private sector involved? What were their roles?

G. Was this negotiation to be part of a larger negotiating process? If so, what linkage with that process was necessary?

H. In the US were the US Congress, the White House or other agencies of the Executive Branch involved? Were there legislative restraints on the US team? How was the domestic political base for the negotiations established in the other countries involved?

I. Were the media aware of these preparations? Were they a factor to be reckoned with?

J. How did the parties structure themselves to prepare for the negotiations? Did the US establish an in-house secretariat? Who was in charge? How were position papers written and cleared? Who developed the US Scope Paper outlining US policy, goals and objectives for the negotiations?

K. Who were the principal negotiators — what was their background, their experience with the subject? Who made up the negotiating teams? How were they selected? Were the teams politically 'balanced'? How much authority did each team have — how much flexibility? What was the chain of command to headquarters? Who wrote the instructions — could other channels of communication be used?

L. Were the negotiating teams well briefed before the negotiations started? Had members of individual teams worked together before? Had the teams worked out in advance proposals or counter-proposals; in other words were they ready to start talking when they sat down at the conference table?

M. Were cultural differences between the parties understood by the US team? Had they been taken into account? Were languages a problem? Were the teams staffed to cope with language differences? Were simultaneous interpreters used?

N.   What informal contacts were made between parties during this preparatory phase? Had friends and allies of the US been adequately informed of the US positions? Did they understand and support the US or were they indifferent or even hostile? Did the United Nations play a role?

O.   How long was this preparatory phase?

III.   The Negotiations Themselves

A.   Were there opening ceremonies? If so did they have any impact on the mood or on the substance of the meeting?

B.   Who actually attended? Was there a credentials problem? Were there unexpected observers? Who were the key players? What were their respective roles?

C.   Was the meeting open to the public? What was the role of the media?

D.   How was the chairman, president or mediator chosen? Were his powers agreed upon in advance? Was the chairmanship rotated? Were there other officers appointed or elected? What kind of a conference record was kept; by whom?

E.   Was there a conference secretariat? What was its role? How was it formed; was it biased? Who paid for the secretariat and the other conference services?

F.   Was there an agenda? Had it been agreed upon during stages I or II? If there was no agenda, how were the issues handled; were the easy items taken first or last?

G.   Explain the formal conference structure. Was there also an informal structure? How did they interrelate? Were there committees, drafting groups, etc.? Was the structure used to the advantage of one or all parties? Did the structure help to achieve a constructive outcome?

H.   Describe the setting, the atmosphere and the dynamics of the negotiation. Explain the ebb and flow, the peaks and valleys of the meeting. Many conferences start with enthusiasm, and high expectations, then go downhill as reality sets in and positions become more widely known, then rise towards the end of the negotiation. Was there a pattern in this negotiation? Was that pattern predicted by the US team?

I.   Describe the tactics that were used as each party revealed its initial positions; its fall-back positions. Did the parties clearly and openly define their interests and objectives? Was pressure used to achieve goals? Were subterfuges used?

J.   How much flexibility was built into the instructions? Was there actual give and take at the conference table by the negotiators or were all signals rigidly controlled by headquarters?

K.   Was the geographical group system used? What communications techniques were used between groups and negotiating teams? Did US tactics vary when dealing with friendly or unfriendly parties?

L.   What were the intra-team dynamics? How did the US team handle international policy disagreements? Were daily team staff meetings used?

M.   How was US communications with headquarters organized? Did the US have formal telegraphic reporting requirements? How was the telephone used; the back channel? Was headquarters back-stopping adequate? How was it structured?

N.   Were US representation funds adequate to do the job? Were they used with skill? How did other teams, observers, etc., do in this area?

O.   How important was the factor of time in reaching a conclusion? If the negotiation was scheduled to end on a certain date was this deadline honoured? Did the parties use the clock as a negotiating tool?

P.   Were the parties able to change each other's original positions? What concessions, real or perceived, were made by each party? Had instructions been exceeded?

Q.   Was this a costly negotiation in policy terms — in dollar terms? Were financial or human resources committed in order to reach agreement? Was the lack of US resources a factor in the final outcome?

R.   Was it possible to conclude the negotiations in one session? Did deadlines play a role?

S.   What closure tactics were used in reaching consensus? Was there a vote?

T.   How flexible and innovative were the various parties? How effective and skilful were the negotiators; the teams?

U.   If negotiations were not concluded, what were the reasons for this? Was any one team at fault? Who was blamed publicly, privately, for failure?

V.   How was the final conference report handled? Was there a communiqué? Was the ending an emotional one?

W.   What was the media's role on the outcome of the negotiations?

IV.   The Post-Negotiation Period

A.   Did headquarters understand and agree with the outcome? Did they believe they had been kept fully informed?

B.   How many of the original US goals and objectives were achieved? Were the strategies and tactics planned in the earlier stages seen as the right ones?

C.   Was a comprehensive final report filed with headquarters by the team leader?

D.   If negotiations were not completed, were de-briefings held within the US government to analyse why this had happened? Was a determination made to hold another round of negotiations?

E.   If negotiations were completed, were de-briefings held to determine the next steps that should be taken to carry out the agreements negotiated?

F.   What was the role of the US negotiating team in helping to insure implementation of the agreed-upon recommendations?

G.   What had to be done to ensure implementation? Was the White House involved? Was action by the Executive Branch all that was required or would the Congress have to be involved? Was domestic legislation necessary? Would the treaty ratification process be involved?

H.   What domestic groups approved implementation of the negotiations? Were other groups in opposition? Was this dissent predicted?

I.   Did the other parties to the negotiation have difficulty in implementing the recommendations for action?

J.   Were any issues in the negotiation left unresolved that might jeopardize implementation? How long could one expect this negotiated settlement to last? How firm or fragile was it?

K.   What lessons for future negotiators can be learned from this case study about the art of negotiation? In brief, why was it successful or unsuccessful?

OBSERVATIONS

It seems that I am the only Track I practitioner included in this compendium. Acknowledging therefore that my perspective will be a bit different, I would like to make a few comments about several of the earlier chapters of this book.

I agree with Michael Banks when he says 'there is a developing gap between theory and practice' and 'there is a disjunction between what the academics say and what the practitioners are doing'. He goes on to point out that the practitioner often ignores the academic because of the latter's paucity of ideas with regard to long-range thinking and global strategy. If it was news to the academic community ten years ago that states are heavily influenced 'by the internal mechanisms of bureaucratic politics' and today that 'states are anything but unitary rational actors', then the study of conflict resolution has a long way to go before it can help a practitioner. I learned these truths in 1947, after three months in the government.

Perhaps a series of two-way exchange programmes, between the US government and universities interested in the area of conflict management, could be a step towards narrowing this experience gap. The Center for the Study of Foreign Affairs now has one Scholar-in-Residence position which is intended to make a beginning in this direction. The recently authorized US Institute for Peace could make an important contribution in this field.

Ed Azar's ten propositions on protracted social conflict are outstanding. Practical, hard-hitting and to the point they send a clear message that any negotiator can understand. I particularly appreciated his comment that the real source of conflict was the denial of those human needs that are common to us all, and his statement that conflict resolution involved far more than conflict management.

John Burton's contributions are always impressive. The concept that certain values are non-negotiable, while other interests can be traded, is a particularly perceptive insight. Every negotiator should try to identify and understand those values and those interests before embarking on a negotiation.

Burton's chapter on process is extremely helpful even though I disagree with his statement that the term *negotiation* should be confined to the final stages of settlement. He has shown how Track II efforts can be more effectively structured for greater impact. His concept and definition of a facilitator is important. This whole chapter, in fact, represents a major contribution to the process of conflict resolution.

As a practitioner, I have great difficulty with Anthony Smith's approach. His frustration over the nation-state is understandable but his move to an 'inter-communalist' approach in order to resolve conflict is unrealistic. 'The international community', absent a world government, is not in a position to manage or negotiate these suggested changes. As Smith himself states, this shift to the communal level could in fact 'increase the potential for conflict ten or one-hundred fold, particularly in Asia and Africa'.

In 1970, the State Department foresaw the creation of a number of new mini-states (e.g. the Seychelles — 70,000 people), all of whom would seek, as their first priority, membership in the United Nations. In an effort to maintain the sanctity of the one-state–one-vote concept, the Department proposed to the United Nations that a new category of membership be created — an associate member. Each state in the category would pay no dues to the United Nations, would have full access to all services, including technical assistance, and could speak and circulate proposals at all meetings. The new state, however, could not vote. This very rational and practical proposal, from our point of view, fell on deaf ears; not one government supported the idea and it was dropped. The nation-state still reigns supreme today.

CONCLUSION

This excellent book contains a number of stimulating ideas and suggestions and should help to narrow the gap between the academic and the practitioner. It focuses mainly on Track II efforts to reduce physical conflict at the community level.

Perhaps, in the future, more attention could be given to bilateral and multilateral conflict between states. Efforts should be made to move towards the peaceful resolution of political disputes by building on economic, social and cultural agreements.

NOTES

1. *International Negotiations: Art and Science* (1984) — Center for the Study of Foreign Affairs — Department of State.
2. *How to be a Delegate* (1984) — Center for the Study of Foreign Affairs –Department of State.
3. *Foreign Policy*, no. 45, Winter 81–2.

Selected Bibliography

Alger, Chadwick F. (1981) 'Creating participatory global cultures', *Alternatives*, **4**, No.4.

Azar, Edward E. (1979) 'Peace amidst development. A conceptual agenda for conflict and peace research'. *International Interactions*, **6**, No.2. New York: Gordon and Breach Science Publications Inc.

Azar, Edward E., and Farah, Nadia (1981) 'The structure of inequalities and protracted social conflict'. *International Interactions*, **7**, No.4.

Banks, Michael (ed.) (1984) *Conflict in World Society. A New Perspective on International Relations*. Brighton, UK: Harvester Press; New York: St Martins.

Barkun, Michael (1970) *Law Without Sanctions*. Princeton, NJ: Princeton University Press.

Burton, John W. (1969) *Conflict and Communication. The Use of Controlled Communications in International Relations*. London: Macmillan.

Burton, John W. (1972) *World Society*. London and New York: Cambridge University Press.

Burton, John W. (1979) *Deviance, Terrorism and War. The Process of Solving Unsolved Social and Political Problems*. Oxford: Martin Robertson; New York: St Martins.

Burton, John W. (1984) *Global Conflict. The Domestic Sources of International Crisis*. Brighton, UK: Wheatsheaf; Center for International Development, University of Maryland, USA.

Cohen, Stephen P., Kelman, Herbert C., Miller, Frederick D. and Smith, Bruce L. (1977) 'Evolving intergroup techniques for conflict resolution: an Israeli-Palestinian pilot workshop', *Journal of Social Issues*, **33**, No.1.

Mitchell, C.R. (1981) *Peacemaking and the Consultant's Role*. London: Gower; New York: Nichols Publishing Co.

Mitchell, C.R. (1981) *The Structure of International Conflict*. London: Macmillan Press Ltd.

Sites, Paul (1973) *Control: the Basis of Social Order*. New York: Dunellen.

Index

vocabulary of, 11
Popper, Karl, 49, 50
Power politics, 42, 111
Power sharing, 34
Practice and theory, 5-11
Primordialism, 68-73
Problem solving, 44, 45, 85-91, 95-7
  in practice, 126-40
  procedures of, 106-7
Problems, origins of, 117
Protracted conflicts, 29-39
Psychology, 56-62, 78

Quebec, 76

Radical thinking, 13
Raiffa, Howard, 142
Ramberg, B., 18
Rapoport, Anatol, 21
Rationalization, 22
Realism, 6, 17, 25
Realist-idealist debate, 9-13
Recognition, human need for, 29, 59-60, 74
Re-entry problem, 108, 129
Reform, 23
Reformist interventionism, 8
Religion, 67
Resolution of conflict, 33-4, 38, 85-91, 94-7, 98-100, 124-5
  in practice, 126-40
Richardson thesis, 38
Rosenau, James, 18, 20
Rousseau, J.-J., 13

St Pierre, 13
Saunders, Hal, 142
Scholars *See* Academics
Schumpeter, 13
Science, philosophy of, 49
Scuttling, 89
Scientific research, 14

Security as human need, 29, 74, 131
Security Council, UN, 43, 45
Self-esteem, 57
Self-image, 33
Self, psychology of, 56-62
Seminars, 86
  on Lebanon conflict, 126-40
Settlement of conflicts, 52, 86, 94-8
Shepard, H.A., 44
Shuttle diplomacy, 101
Singer, J. David, 20
Sites, Paul, 48, 51
Smith, Anthony, 63-80
Snyder, Richard, 18
Social goals, 99
Sohn, Louis, 142
Solutions, 78-80
  See also Resolution of conflict
South Africa, 99
Sovereignty, 10, 31, 60
Soviet Union, 54, 121-2, 123-4
  and USA, 117-21
Sri Lanka, 37, 76
State
  as cause of wars, 64
  nature of, 19
  nation-, *see* nation-states
  as political norm, 77
State-nations, 71
Stewart, Prof. P.D., 144
Structuralism, 7, 17
Susskind, Larry, 142
Symbols, 60
Symposium on International Negotiation, 142

Terrorism, 59, 139
Theory and practice, 5-11
Third party in conflict analysis, 103, 104-5